PRAISE FOR *GOLF ETIQUETTE*

"You must learn the etiquette of golf. . . . My suggestion is to buy and memorize a book called *Golf Etiquette,* which is written by my longtime friend and pupil Barbara Puett with help from Jim Apfelbaum. . . . If you observe the rules of etiquette and play promptly, you will always be a welcome golfing companion, regardless of your handicap."

—**Harvey Penick**
Golf Professional Emeritus
Austin Country Club

"Filled with tips applicable to everyone from the beginner to the less-than-couth low handicapper . . . Besides making you better prepared, *Golf Etiquette* will make you a more pleasant partner. Rating: ****"

—*Golf* **magazine**

"In the past I've been known to play thirty-six and fifty-four holes a day, and know the meaning of pace of play. This book teaches golfers how to do it: when to walk, when to talk, and how to keep up, how to be a more enjoyable partner. Slow play wouldn't be the problem it's become if everyone read this book."

—**Darrell Royal**

"*Golf Etiquette*, the first and last word on how properly to behave on and off the golf course."

—**Paul Harvey**

GOLF
ETIQUETTE

Revised Edition

GOLF
ETIQUETTE

Revised Edition

Barbara Puett
and
Jim Apfelbaum

St. Martin's Press ❧ New York

GOLF ETIQUETTE, REVISED EDITION. Copyright © 2003 by Barbara Puett and Jim Apfelbaum. Foreword copyright © 2003 by Ben Crenshaw. Introduction copyright © 2003 by Tom Kite. All rights reserved. Printed in the United States of America. No part of this book may be used or reproduced in any manner whatsoever without written permission except in the case of brief quotations embodied in critical articles or reviews. For information, address St. Martin's Press, 175 Fifth Avenue, New York, N.Y. 10010.

Photographs © 2003 by Ralph Barrera
Illustrations © 2003 by Eddy Davis

www.stmartins.com

Library of Congress Cataloging-in-Publication Data

Puett, Barbara.
    Golf etiquette / Barbara Puett and Jim Apfelbaum.—Rev. ed.
      p. cm.
    Includes bibliographical references (p. 179).
    ISBN 0-312-30647-4
    1. Golf. 2. Etiquette. I. Apfelbaum, Jim. II. Title.

  GV965.P84 2003
  796.352—dc21

                                                    2003053850

First Edition: November 2003

10 9 8 7 6 5 4 3 2 1

CONTENTS

FOREWORD by Ben Crenshaw   vii

INTRODUCTION by Tom Kite   ix

PREFACE TO THE SECOND EDITION   xi

ONE: ON THE DRIVING RANGE AND PRACTICE
PUTTING GREEN   1

TWO: WHAT TO WEAR   14

THREE: PREPARING TO PLAY   26

FOUR: ON THE TEE   33

FIVE: ON THE FAIRWAY   50

SIX: IN A WATER, SAND, OR LATERAL HAZARD   70

SEVEN: ON THE GREEN   79

EIGHT: KEEPING SCORE   94

NINE: GOLF RULES YOU SHOULD KNOW   100

TEN: PLAYING IN A TOURNAMENT   111

ELEVEN: BUSINESS GOLF   120

TWELVE: RESORT GOLF   138

THIRTEEN: EQUIPMENT   149

FOURTEEN: TAKING LESSONS   163

A QUICK DEFINITION OF TERMS	171
BETTER PLAYERS AND NEW GOLFERS	175
GOLF ETIQUETTE'S 10 *LEAST* WANTED LIST	177
COMMENCEMENT ADDRESS	178
READING LIST	179
ABOUT THE AUTHORS	181
INDEX	183

FOREWORD

Golf etiquette is an imbedded tradition that is nearly as much a part of the game as the play itself.

Throughout golf's history it has been customary to treat your opponent or playing companions with due consideration. In other words, when someone says to you, "It is your honor" to play, it represents more than mere procedure. In simple terms it means that one is expected to be on his or her best behavior when on the golf course.

Respect for the rules, the golf course, and the player ensures a consistent future for a pastime that has endured for more than five hundred years.

It is helpful that books such as *Golf Etiquette* should be introduced to golfers of all ages. It is up to all of us to keep these wonderful traditions alive to provide new generations a chance to enjoy the game that so many of us have enjoyed all these years.

BEN CRENSHAW

INTRODUCTION

Most of us who consider ourselves golfers have at one time or another been confounded and confused by the Rules of Golf. Some even consider the Rule Book to be too lengthy or not appropriate for today's game or just too much of a bother. After all, they say, the game is difficult enough without having to play by the strictest of rules.

But one part of the rules that should not be ignored by anyone who wishes to have someone else to play with is the Rules of Etiquette. Obviously the USGA, the rule-making body, feels that proper golf etiquette is important. That is why they chose to put some suggestions at the front of every Rule Book.

And as the game continues to grow in popularity, the Rules of Etiquette become even more important. They are what separates golf from other sports and allows all players of different handicap levels to have a good time, even on the days the putts don't drop.

This book is long overdue. If this were a college course, it would be must reading. And whether or not you have the inclination and courage to wade through the Rules of Golf, reading and abiding by *Golf Etiquette* will help ensure that you and your playing partners will always enjoy golf.

TOM KITE

Both Tom and Ben, in addition to their exceptional competitive careers, have each been honored by the USGA as recipients of the Bob Jones Award, given to those who show "respect for the game and its rules, a generosity of spirit, a sense of fair play, self-control and perhaps even self-sacrifice . . . summed up in the word 'sportsmanship.' " Thank you again, gentlemen, for your contributions.

PREFACE TO THE SECOND EDITION

"Golf is, in part, a game; but only in part. It is also in part a religion, a fever, a vice, a mirage, a frenzy, a fear, an abscess, a joy, a thrill, a pest, a disease, an uplift, a brooding, a melancholy, a dream of yesterday, and a hope for tomorrow."

—*New York Tribune* (1916)

Slow play remains golf's number-one problem. It's rude and arrogant to be a slow player, even if it's unintentional. Many golfers fail to realize that their best opportunity to hit their best shot comes in playing quickly.

Golf etiquette refers to the game's "unwritten rules" of decorum. Pace of play is an important facet of that code. An old-fashioned word, etiquette may be a Victorian hand-me-down, evocative, perhaps, of a prim and proper time that bears little resemblance to today.

Nothing could be further from the truth. Etiquette is about mindfulness, consideration, and attitude. The game cannot survive without it. Proper etiquette demonstrates awareness and respect for the environment, for the game and for others. All those who practice it share a bond.

One of Barbara's students put it succinctly: "It's not how good you are, but how good you are to play with." That sentiment is echoed by early British champion Abe Mitchell, who wrote: "The sum total of the rules [of etiquette] is thoughtfulness." Exactly.

In a game of uncertainty, etiquette offers an island of common sense and safety. It continues to evolve along with the game, which explains this new and updated edition. Learning the game's manners, perplexing at first, may be golf's easiest and most enduring lesson.

Etiquette still matters. As golf continues to welcome new devotees, etiquette takes on ever more significance. Thank you for taking the time to preserve the venerable tradition that connects all golfers to the game's past and its future.

> "I can't think of anything that would lend itself more to the enjoyment of the game than knowing the Rules of Etiquette."
>
> —Harvey Penick

GOLF
ETIQUETTE

Revised Edition

1 ON THE DRIVING RANGE AND PRACTICE PUTTING GREEN

"Everyone has had the experience and knows how annoying it is hearing the swish of a club behind him just as he is in the midst of his swing. He has to be very fond of the culprit to restrain a desire to bash him on the head with the club, even when he knows that the guilt is only of thoughtlessness."

—Bob Jones, *Bobby Jones on Golf*

To the uninitiated, golf can be as unfamiliar as a foreign country. Etiquette serves as golf's passport. Learn the game's ethical code and you'll be accepted wherever golf is played. Etiquette answers a lot of questions. It's the key to understanding and appreciating golf's rich traditions, culture, and customs. Safety remains etiquette's primary concern, never more important than on the driving range. Here, as on the golf course, accepted protocol establishes a sense of order, comfort, and rhythm that ideally carries over from practice to play.

One thing that doesn't change: people. You'll notice that those oblivious to the game's manners are the same folks who park illegally, blab away on cell phones, and cut you off in traffic. The driving range may offer a first brush with golf—

and with those blissfully unaware of convention and common sense. For those who have lives, jobs, and families, stealing four hours of daylight to play golf can be a rarity, but there are ways to creatively slip in a few minutes of practice at lunch, after work, or as a diversion on a business trip. Practice provides an evening's entertainment alone or shared with friends and family or even newly made acquaintances. Ranges may also offer a place to eat, take a lesson, or shop for clothing or equipment.

HOW OTHERS DO IT

Anyone paying a green fee can walk onto a public golf course in the United States and tee it up. That's not the case across the globe. Many countries have procedures that ease golfers into the game, etiquette included, and new golfers are required to make the effort.

In Sweden, for example, admittance to a golf course requires every player to first demonstrate proficiency as well as a basic understanding of the rules and etiquette. A sample quiz appears at the end of the chapter.

BUDDY, CAN YOU SPARE A 5-IRON

Clubs are not required to use the range. Manufacturer's "demos" or loaner clubs will likely be available for those without their own. Expect to leave a credit card or a driver's license as a deposit.

A LARGE BUCKET TO GO

The good news with range balls is that you won't have to pick them up or return them. Just leave the bucket or bag when you're done. At country clubs or high-end daily fee courses, range balls are often included in the green fee. Help yourself to any freebies left behind. They may look like real golf balls, but range balls fly shorter distances. It makes them easier to collect and less attractive to thieves.

Set up your practice pile so that with a simple flick of the club a new ball can be scooted into place. Remedial as this may seem, doing it this way allows efficiency in movement without having to step back to snag a new ball each time. This provides a measure of safety when no divider separates golfers. The balls in front serve as a barrier for the unthinking golfer backing into your space who risks being hit by a swinging club.

Resort ranges often attractively stack range balls in pyramids. (There's a plastic form; no one does this by hand.) Even when the balls are not so decoratively displayed, they should be stored or positioned between you and the next person over.

Everyone should be evenly spaced along the same line.

YOU MAY FIRE WHEN READY

Ranges commonly offer golf bag stands or provide some definition for the individual hitting areas with stakes, boards, or mats. Even when there's just a rope on the ground, place the bag behind the hitting area. No one will care if you do it some other way, but it will peg you as a newcomer. A bag directly behind a practicing golfer tells passersby to walk around.

Two ropes on the ground commonly mark the hitting zone. (If there's only one, always set up behind it.) Boundaries are routinely shifted up and back to spare the grass. Doing so also alters the posted distance to the targets. Regardless of what others are doing, position yourself inside the ropes or within the defined hitting area.

There will always be those who choose to hit off grass even when posted signs prohibit it, or prefer to play from beyond the ropes. Watch out for golfers hitting at awkward angles. Remain within the guidelines, making certain that others have not positioned themselves in a way that places you even indirectly in their line of fire. *For safety's sake, everyone should be evenly spaced along the same line.* Country club pros don't relish correcting their members, nor do driving ranges enjoy admonishing their customers, so little is likely to be said when someone lines up improperly. Resist the temptation to venture out into the live minefield, even a few steps, to retrieve a ball or tee. Some ranges have mats or grass tees depending upon the weather conditions or the demands of the season. Some offer a choice. Two things are certain: the grass is always greener and fuller down at the far end of the range and, at some point, bag on your shoulder, balls teetering in the basket, a few will topple out.

○ The one place where divots can be blithely overlooked? The driving range.

Between the markers, behind the rope, balls easily within reach.

CAUTION: GOLFERS AT WORK

Some ranges set aside room for those taking lessons from the facility's staff. Posted signs will alert golfers to avoid these or any other restricted areas.

STRIKING WHEN THE IRON'S HOT

When the range is small or maintenance is in progress, signs will insist that only irons be practiced. Perhaps long drives will endanger golfers or passing traffic, or they could imperil or interfere with repairs. Whatever the reason, if that's the policy, the directive must be observed.

IF YOU'D LIKE TO MAKE A CALL

Ah, reality's dulcet ringing reminder intruding on the casual atmosphere of the practice range. Sure, we're not on the golf course. True, there's no competition in progress. Undoubtedly it's an important call: a sales lead, your playing partner is caught in traffic, a child forgot her lunch money. Sorry. The driving range is no different than the library, restaurant, movie theater, or golf course. Move away with the phone or at least stay away from those trying to steal a few minutes' diversion. Those disapproving looks are not because of your swing. Put the thing, turn the ringer, keep your voice—*down*. It's rude. It's a distraction. You might offer a quick apology to those studiously practicing.

The social informality of the range masks a genuine purpose. Improvement requires those old standbys: diligence and concentration. Can we agree that learning is best accomplished with a minimum of noise and distraction? You may do the taxes with the TV on. You may have been one of those prodigies who could study with the stereo blaring. *That* was in the privacy of your own home. Out of consideration for others, back away from the hitting stations or go to the end of the range.

○ Hi! Yeah, it's me. I'm at the golf course. Blah, blah, blah, blah.

There is a joke about the cellular invasion in golf. A golfer hears ringing on his backswing and announces, "I can hit a cell phone 230 [yards]." Best not to tempt anyone. Everyone on the driving range has an agenda; some will be quite serious, others are just loosening up. All deserve deference.

PLAYTIME

Golf is an activity happily enjoyed regardless of age. How lovely that you're sharing it with your kids. We're delighted, and no one ever objects to a well-mannered child. A rise over a show of inappropriate behavior can be expected at a restaurant or movie, and you can also expect it around the range, where the same standards of public civility, declining or not, still apply. There are also legitimate safety concerns. Small children should not be allowed free rein. Once again, that empty area down at the end of the range offers more freedom. Sand traps (or, as golfers technically and correctly refer to them, bunkers) are not sand boxes. Two thoughts: perhaps there's another unoccupied bunker nearby. There is always the putting green, which welcomes all who demonstrate consideration, and where youth can hone a decided advantage. Putting comes more easily to children. A golf course can seem a huge, intimidating expanse, but the practice green is on a more comforting, child-sized, and child-friendly scale.

The parent-child golf lesson is another potential point of contention. Our research shows that golfers find loud, punitive instruction from parents about as pleasant as listening to half of an animated cell phone conversation. Please keep your voices down when training your Tiger. The great thing about driving ranges is their expanse. They allow plenty of room for a golfer to be alone with his (swing) thoughts. And did you happen to notice the empty space down at the far end? That's where the golf pro gives lessons, wisely recognizing the value of removing students from the fray. Why not move down that way if the range is crowded?

YOU GET WHAT YOU PAY FOR ("TIPS")

Beginners, especially women, are easy prey for swing instruction on the range, often innocently disguised as "tips." The very nature of practice reveals a vulnerability in golfers that some people can't resist; one's inexperience is exposed, out in the open for all to see. A "real" lesson from a competent instructor will supply the resolve, if not to put the good-intentioned "helper" in his place, then to at least persuade him to search elsewhere for a weaker member of the herd. A firm "Thanks, but I'm working on something" should be enough to curtail the interruption.

A TURN ON THE "DANCE FLOOR"

Every golf course has a practice putting green; they're free to use. Occasionally, stand-alone ranges will insist upon the purchase of a bucket of balls to allow access to the green. Otherwise no payment is required. Practice before or after a round, or whenever the mood strikes, as many do on the fly, leisurely honing this most important and delicate skill. High heels, whether on clunky loafers or boots, from high-fashion to cowboy, should remain on the sidelines. Anything that will leave an indentation should never traverse the green's smooth surface. Bare feet or socks are preferable to damaging treads or heels. It's a rare occurrence, committed by the unknowing, but worth mentioning. Sneakers are fine. And if you're not using the green, walk around it.

○ Putt with real golf balls on the practice green, even if range balls are scattered nearby.

HELLO, IT'S ME

Some clubs have banned cell phones outright, others disallow them on the driving range or inside the clubhouse. Spectators can no longer bring them into PGA Tour events. For those practicing their putting, their nuisance value remains high. Even though the practice green is a casual setting, turn the volume down or put it on vibrate. Leave the green to take a call. You'll have the privacy the call merits without creating a distraction.

"Long putts travel on the wings of chance."
—Bernard Darwin, *Wise Words for Golfers*

Putt with real balls. Share the holes when it's crowded.

PUTTING FOR SHOW

On a crowded green share the holes. There's no traffic pattern. When the green is not full, everyone generally spreads out, or moves around to practice putts of different character and length.

Move far enough away from the hole you've just finished before you resume putting. Standing too close needlessly monopolizes two holes and unnecessarily imperils the fragile area near the cup.

When the green's

especially crowded, putt from shorter distances, or stick a tee in the ground in an area of the green without a hole and putt to it. Always be gentle removing and replacing flagsticks.

A CHIP AND A PUTT

It's OK to chip (hit short shots to a hole from just off the green) unless a sign prohibits doing so. Apply common sense and safety. When the green is crowded, confine practice to the closer holes. Chipping from across the green puts everyone on the alert. No one should have to do an evasive two-step to avoid an errant shot. It happens all too often. Inexperienced golfers haven't yet learned how far back to take the club to hit short-range shots. Occasionally a fast-moving projectile is launched. Needless to say, "beaning" another golfer is a breach of etiquette. Few things are more embarrassing than a sculled shot on a crowded green followed by a plaintive cry of "Fore!"

THE PITTER-PATTER OF LITTLE FEET

The practice green is a great place to introduce kids to golf. Little feet running certainly won't damage a putting green, but learning early not to run on the green is a terrific introduction to etiquette. Little children can also be made aware that golf bags, pull carts (even kid-sized pull carts, bags, and strollers) are best left to the side of the practice green.

BRIEFING

• On the range, hit from between the guide ropes; always stay behind the single rope on the ground that defines the hitting area. Place your bag directly behind you, a "Golfers Working" sign to those passing by.

• Keep an eye on others, particularly those ignoring the unwritten rules of the range. Make darn sure you're not in their line of fire. Everyone practicing should be relatively even along the line defined by the ropes or hitting stations.

• Turn down that cell phone ringer. Keep your voice down. Back away from the hitting stations and try and be as unobtrusive as possible. Some clubs ban cell phones from the range, and even inside the clubhouse. Step away from the putting green so others can putt in peace.

• Take kids to the less crowded area down at the end, where the turf is always better. The practice green is also a great place to start kids out with putting and to share the concept of good manners.

• Always chip to the closest hole when the green's crowded. Beware golfers practicing too difficult or adventurous shots.

• Heels of any kind are not permitted on putting greens.

• Step far enough away from the hole you've just finished before taking aim again.

○ From *Rules and Tests for Green Card in Sweden, 1999*

Golf Etiquette

a. What are the colors of the tees?
b. What are you supposed to do when you hear someone shout FORE?
c. Name four examples of how to save time on the course.
d. Name three reasons to let the following party pass.
e. Where shall you stand when your partner plays a shot?
f. Why are you expected to replace a divot?
g. What are you expected to do before you leave a bunker?
h. Why are you expected to repair a pitch-mark on the green?

Courtesy Swedish Golf Federation

The Ladies' Golf Association of the Austin (TX) Country Club,
circa 1933, appropriately dressed.

2 WHAT TO WEAR

"One must be comfortable to execute correctly the movements of the golf swing. Shots call for concentration, so if the golfer is properly attired, he need not worry about this or that being out of place, which is bound to distract his mind from the shot. Designers have noted that clothes for golf should be loose fitting, and have added pleats here and there so that the player will be comfortable, and thus be enabled to get freedom in the swing."

—Sam Snead, *How to Play Golf* (1946)

"How on earth any one of us ever managed to hit a ball, or get along at all in the outrageous garments with which fashion decreed we were to cover ourselves, is one of the great unsolved mysteries of that or any age."

—Mabel E. Stringer, *Golfing Reminiscences* (1924)

There are rules of thumb to dressing a good game. These depend upon the setting, the situation, even the region. With ample room for personal expression, the burden falls to the individual to determine what's appropriate and to dress accordingly.

It could be mercerized cotton, marled yarns, or silk blends, a knit vest of smoky plum accented with an antique rich cinnamon and gray charcoal, or a classic navy and cream polo with sporty marine blue accents. Whatever your personal preference, every department store, from mall anchor to deep discount, sells clothes appropriate for golf. Most "work" as well off the course. Often noted in invitation parlance as "country club casual," or "golf casual," the description is indicative of golf's wider acceptance.

DRESSING A GOOD GAME

On public courses, those owned and operated by city or state recreation departments, acceptable dress is constrained only by statutes of public decency. A course charging $10 or $20 is unlikely to expect more than shirts, shoes, and, presumably, pants. Golf shoes are no longer mandatory, but high heels, boots, or *any* footwear that could damage a green, are prohibited. Riding along in the cart, an unsuspecting non-golfing companion will occasionally step onto a green unaware of the consequences and the tender loving care required to restore and maintain greens. This obviously should be avoided.

Most courses insist that men keep their shirts on, a prudent policy based as much on health concerns as to avoid traumatizing half their customers.

TAKE NOTHING FOR GRANTED

Golf courses follow a roughly drawn hierarchy, from city-owned to privately owned public courses to various levels of private country clubs. There are notable exceptions, but generally the further up the ladder one plays, the more expensive the course, the better condition it's in, and the more attention that is paid to ancillary matters like shorts and jeans.

On municipal courses denim may be allowed, although cutoffs are best avoided. A man playing golf in a Speedo and an old pair of sneakers would seem an unlikely sight, especially on a top resort course. Albeit an extreme contravention of apparel standards, the haunting image remains with those who bore witness. Just as some courses permit walking while others prohibit it, dress codes vary. Assume nothing. Call the pro shop with concerns or questions.

COLLARED

"Semiprivate" courses (also called daily-fee) welcome public play. These mostly constitute the better grade of public course with fees ranging from around $40 to well over $200. Pebble Beach Golf Links, along California's spectacular Monterey Peninsula, is often hailed as an exceptional "public" course, which it certainly is, as open to the public as Maxim's in Paris or any other famous (and famously expensive) restaurant; to anyone that is, in Pebble Beach's case, willing to part with $350 (plus cart). That's the current green fee for one turn around the famous links. And there's no shortage of takers. Appropriate attire at Pebble would be acceptable anywhere: a collared shirt with slacks or walking shorts. No blue jeans.

Collarless, sleeveless, denim shorts—appropriate only for municipal courses.

Whoa, dude. Perfect for muny courses but not for semiprivate or country clubs.

Many semiprivate courses pride themselves on offering the "country club for a day experience." Dress codes are common (and they go double for nongolfing companions, who may also be charged a cart fee).

A collar is routinely required on shirts for men, universally accepted on those worn by women. Denim, again, is iffy and best avoided. No statistics are available, but courses must make a tidy sum selling golf shirts along with a green fee to those arriving at better courses unaware of their policy. Some private clubs ban colored denim, which would also cover variations like black, patterned, and beige jeans. To avoid any embarrassment, ask ahead of time.

WHO WEARS SHORT SHORTS?

Shorts of varying lengths are another area of uncertainty. Men may (we keep saying "some courses *may* permit this" and "some courses may allow that" because the policies vary so widely) be required to don "walking" length shorts. Women typically need shorts that fall four inches above the knee.

Appropriate anywhere.

Styles change, as do hemlines, requirements, and club directors. We've focused on traditional golf attire, but there's no telling how fashions may evolve. We are more than confident in suggesting the following be stricken from any budding golf wardrobe:

- running shorts
- halter tops
- T-shirts (bearing devotional slogans to colleges, endangered species, etc.)
- cutoffs
- cutoff shirts
- swimwear
- sweat suits
- tank tops
- crop tops
- short shorts
- jeans (any color)
- shoes with metal cleats (another indication of how times change)

You may likely encounter someone wearing any of the preceding items (even, shudder, a guy in a tight Speedo) but it's best to adhere to convention.

AT THE CLUB

Now it really gets interesting because country club dress codes vary as widely as initiation fees. Those who have no intention of joining a private club should nevertheless be aware that playing in a charity event hosted by a club will require adhering to their definition of appropriate. Also, members inviting guests to play can become so accustomed to club policy that they forget to tip off their friends. Again, any doubts can be discreetly allayed over the phone.

Trying to divine a course's dress code by its name is an exercise in futility. Just because it has "country club" in the name doesn't mean the course is even private, let alone provide an inkling of the policies on attire.

Ditto. Note the length of the shorts.

BOTTOM LINE

Generally acceptable anywhere:

For men
Collared shirts
Slacks or walking shorts

For women
    Collared shirts
    Shorts four inches above the knee

That said, nothing is ever simple with women's fashions. Some courses ban T-shirts, for instance, but a growing number allow them as part of a matching outfit. Then again, many charity events hand out T-shirts as prizes, so presumably on those courses T-shirts are welcome.

Sleeveless shirts may also be borderline. Where a collarless shirt with sleeves may be permitted, a sleeveless shirt must have a collar. Shorts are one article of clothing where the (hem) lines are clearly drawn, with length restrictions precise to the inch.

Like tennis, golf fashion goes through evolutionary cycles. You'll be on firm ground remembering that the higher the green fee, or the more exclusive the club, the more serious the scrutiny is over what everyone is wearing. And just to complicate matters for men, some clubs allow collarless shirts provided—here's the kicker—they sport a golf logo. Older, more traditional clubs will have their rules just as the higher-end daily fee (semiprivate) courses, from Pebble Beach on down, have theirs.

An indication of how far dress codes can go comes from a student who recalls being asked to leave the golf shop of a *very* private country club because she was wearing a denim skirt, a contravention of the club's dress code. It mattered not a whit that she was there not to play golf but simply to *buy* something. She was politely asked to leave.

○ In 1977 Nancy Lopez lost the U.S. Open to Hollis Stacy by two strokes after her pants zipper broke. "I was only nineteen," Lopez recalled, "and I was so worried about showing my panties that I couldn't concentrate."
    Moral: Pack a safety pin.

SHORTS STORY

Barbara and Jack Heyde have their own story to tell. They were in Southern Spain. Jack was set to play Valderrama, a renowned course. Barbara decided to ride along with a friend to watch. She had on a nice-looking matching denim shorts outfit. Barbara knew the shorts were a proper length, but she never dreamed the denim would be a problem. It was. She was not allowed on the course, even to watch. She ended up pulling an extra pair of Jack's shorts on over hers. Only then was she permitted out on the golf course.

IF THE SHOE FITS

Golf shoes now look and wear more like real shoes and less like something a nurse might wear on her rounds. Many could serve as stunt doubles for running shoes, cross-trainers, walking shoes, sandals, and even winged tips. They're also much lighter and more comfortable. Most courses expect you'll take advantage and wear them, although requirements have softened as the styles blend.

Some golfers mourn the passing of metal spikes and their pleasing sound, what an industry official once described as their "clackity-clack value." Most courses now require soft cleats (rubber or plastic). Sneakers are fine on most public courses. They've even been worn on the pro circuits. Sneakers (does anyone still call them sneakers?) may be permitted on better courses—some allow them, some don't. If they were seated next to you at the bar, golf shoe manufacturers would stress that golf shoes, unlike sneakers, provide the benefits of continuing technological research and achievement: leather uppers, lightweight flexible outsoles, moisture management, *breathability*, and so on. In other words, they're more durable and more comfortable when the going gets rough.

Sandals expressly designed for golf are another conceivably gray area. The only way to be certain they're allowed on the course you're set to play is to ask. Socks with sandals may be required. Public courses will likely only ask that shoes be flat soled. Those accompanying golfers onto the course, even if they're only riding in the cart, should be aware they fall under the same strictures. No high heels. Likely no boots.

A STIFF UPPER LID

Golfers have been tragically lax about the harmful effects of the sun. Baseball caps and visors, popular though they are, do not provide adequate protection. The brims are not wide enough to shield the ears, neck, or lower face. Important as a safeguard out on the golf course, hats and caps should be removed upon entering the clubhouse; some higher-end courses and clubs do not permit men to wear hats to dine indoors.

WHAT THE PROS WEAR

Professional golfers occasionally stretch convention. Color coordinated and expertly tailored, these high-priced models and billboards are very well compensated. Even T-shirts of a sort, a modified turtleneck without a collar—once unthinkable on a man playing at a top club—now hardly raise an eyebrow when one of the world's best golfers sports one.

The PGA Tour struggles with informality. Pro golfers wear no uniform per se, although there is a dress code. Shorts are expressly prohibited. At present only caddies can show their legs, and this only after several tragic incidents involving heat prostration. Given that shorts are standard in many pro sports, it is hard for some to understand why golf is different, how shorts might somehow tarnish pro golf's image, but that's the way it is. One outspoken opponent of the policy exclaimed: "We should be allowed to wear shorts. God Almighty! Women are allowed to wear them, and we've got better legs than they do."

BRIEFING

• Men should stick to the straight and narrow. The stereotype is threadbare. "Baffling late-life discovery," wrote San Francisco columnist Herb Caen, "golfers wear those awful clothes on purpose." Collared golf shirt, slacks, and golf shoes will always be comfortable, functional with ample room for stylish expression, and accepted anywhere.

• Women should avoid denim, T-shirts, sweat suits, short shorts, jogging or running shorts, tank tops, halter tops, crop tops, cutoffs, or metal cleats. In cold weather, wear sweaters, turtlenecks, and windbreakers—not sweatsuits. Bottom line: Shorts four inches above the knee and collared shirt. The older, more exclusive a club, likely the lower the hemline permitted for shorts.

• A public course does not automatically mean there isn't a dress code.

• Those tagging along with a golfing friend, even if they're only riding around, should observe the golfer's dress code.

• Survey says: "The less skilled the golfer, the more likely he plays in a T-shirt." (*The Darrell Survey*, 2000)

• You've got questions? The pro shop has answers.

○ From the PGA Tour Players' Manual:

1. APPEARANCE OF PLAYERS

Players shall present a neat appearance in both clothing and personal grooming. Clothing worn by players shall be consistent with currently accepted golf fashion. The Tournament Director shall interpret this regulation, subject to the approval of the Commissioner.

3 PREPARING TO PLAY

"The sounds of golf are unique and sweet.
Add to them the smell of the cut grass, the
feel of the sun on your back, the sight of a distant flag waving,
and you can't help but be transported to a better place."
—Gary Player, *The Golfer's Guide to the Meaning of Life*

The Yellow Pages will confirm whether a course welcomes public play. To avoid disappointment, always call before setting out; there may be a tournament under way or they may be closed for maintenance. Green fees, tee time availability, dress codes, walking and pull-cart policies, the likelihood of a single golfer pairing up with others—any question can be answered discreetly in advance, often by e-mail.

TWILIGHT FEES

You might also ask whether the course has a *twilight* fee, a reduced rate for late afternoon play. The course at "low tide" is an ideal time for new players to get acclimated. There may be two twilight fees, one that begins at a certain time of day, adjusted with the change of seasons and daylight. When business is slow, prices often drop to entice golfers. Twilight is also an ideal time to introduce children to golf or to accommodate those who can squeeze in nine holes at dusk. Even with a late starting time, depending upon the season, golfers who hustle can nearly play a full round. On popular courses reservations may be needed.

○ **On some courses Friday is considered a weekend. Green fees are scaled accordingly.**

TEE TIMES

Tee times are not mandatory. They're a reservation, obviously at a premium during peak hours (Saturday and Sunday morning, and holidays). On public courses names are commonly taken from a waiting list to fill in groups of less than four players. Getting on the list will work out fine when you're alone or with a friend; twosomes are easily paired. With less than four players, alert the golf shop in advance so they can begin the jigsaw puzzle of assembling groups. Anyone answering the phone in the golf shop can explain the procedure.

A tee time is golf's equivalent of a flight departure time. It signifies the moment of takeoff. An 8:10 tee time means golfers are assembled on the first tee and the first drive is away at that time. Those who stroll up to the counter two minutes before their scheduled tee time, then head for the snack bar and then back to the parking lot for their clubs, will likely lose their spot. Under similar circumstances they'd never make their flight. That's the way a tee time should be approached. Long before being called to the tee, golfers have to check in, pay, confirm their reservation, and ideally, mentally and physically prepare to play.

Tee times are typically 8 to 10 minutes apart. The pro shop will announce impending departures over a PA system (often at 24-, 16-, and 8-minute intervals leading up to the tee time). It is the golfer's responsibility to be ready.

Every course has its own way of handling tee times. The

stories are legion at big city courses of golfers who sleep out or arrive in the wee hours to get in line. Speed-dialing can come in handy when you are trying to get through to the pro shop to reserve a choice Saturday morning slot. In some cases, you'd stand a better chance of getting through on the radio to win the cash jackpot.

CANCELING A TEE TIME

At busy public courses, no-shows are quickly replaced from a waiting list. At higher-end courses, a 24- or 48-hour cancellation notice policy is common. Reserving a tee time may require a credit card deposit and you may be charged if the cancellation is not phoned in within the grace period.

○ **A tee time is not like a dinner reservation. Your "table" will not be held. There's no such thing as being fashionably late in golf: 8:10 means 8:10, just as it does at the airport. In tournaments, being late is grounds for disqualification.**

ON-TIME ARRIVAL

Arrive a minimum of thirty minutes before your tee time. Courses also have various ways of processing golfers, getting them as expediently as possible from the parking lot to the pro shop to the first tee. Give yourself plenty of time.

At Low-End Daily Fee or Municipal Courses. Take your clubs to the clubhouse door. Place them in the racks provided. Do not take them inside the pro shop when entering to pay. Some courses will have a sign posted to remind golfers not to bring their bags inside. Even if there isn't a sign, the custom is widely followed. Pull carts can be brought or rented.

Some golfers prefer to walk to the pro shop, secure a cart, then drive back to their car to retrieve their clubs. At the end of the round, carts are also commonly driven back to the parking lot to save golfers from having to carry their bag back out before returning the cart. A modest key deposit may also be required and necessitate a trip back to the golf shop to retrieve it.

At High-End Daily Fee Courses or Private and Semiprivate Clubs. A drive-up area may be available (a bag drop) or an attendant will meet you in a cart in the parking lot. He'll assist in escorting you and your clubs to the golf shop. Tip as you might with a baggage handler at the airport. A dollar will suffice. Big tippers will tip more. An attendant will likely meet the group at the end of the round and clean everyone's clubs. A similar tip will be expected.

THE BAG DROP

When no valet service is available, locate the bag drop. Resembling a bicycle rack, it offers a convenient way station to avoid having to carry one's clubs from the farthest reaches of the parking lot up to the pro shop. Double parking to unload is permissible. With a light bag you may simply prefer to park and walk up carrying your bag. If no rack is provided outside the golf shop, just prop the bag against a wall. (Every player must have a bag. Two players may share a set of clubs, divvying up the irons, but each must have a bag and a putter.)

○ **Golfers carrying their bags routinely jettison a few clubs to spare their backs. A fun tournament format allows each player to carry any three, but only three, clubs. There are even one-club events. U.S. Opens have been won with as few as seven clubs.**

SHOES

At Low-End Daily Fee or Municipal Courses. It's OK to put golf shoes on in the parking lot.

At High-End Daily Fee Courses. Permissible to put golf shoes on in the parking lot and stow street shoes in the trunk, the attendant having ferried the clubs up to the shop or placed them in the rack for assignment to a cart.

At Country Clubs or Resort Courses. Carry shoes into the clubhouse (in a shoe bag) and put them on in the locker room. Country club members will have a locker, and guests will leave their street shoes out to be shined. Should that be the case, a tip is appropriate, anywhere from $2 to $5.

STARTER

Having paid your green fee, many courses require one final pre-golf check with the "starter," after which you're good to go. Hold on to the receipt. The starter may ask for it. He'll double-check the names on a list and confirm the starting time. He'll have scorecards and extra pencils, and can offer course recommendations. Appropriate cart policies, pin placements, and any other last-minute tips and instruction will be reviewed. The call over the PA might say: "Smith foursome on the tee, eight minute call for the Carlisle foursome, and we have a sixteen-minute call for the Perez twosome joined by Ellison and Davis. Twenty-four-minute call for the Abel foursome."

At some higher-end courses and private clubs, an access code will be required to enter on-course restrooms. The starter or course rangers will have that code.

"Unlike most other sports, there is no such thing as 'playing defense' in golf. The rules of etiquette stand as a clear proof that golf is primarily about learning to conquer ourselves—our tempers, interior noises, and lapses in concentration—and not about conquering our opponent. Good etiquette means more than being quiet at the proper time, or playing at a reasonable pace; it means giving opponents every opportunity to play their best."   —Roland Merullo, *Passion for Golf*

The best place to wait your turn is alongside, in view, even with
the golfer, and standing still.

4 ON THE TEE

"While a stroke is playing none of the Party shall walk about, make any motion, or attempt to take off the Player's attention, by speaking, or otherwise."   —The Society of Golfers at Aberdeen (1783)

The driving range and practice green are for R&D. *The golf course is for playing golf.* Focus on the game. Visit in the pro shop or after the round. On the golf course the business at hand is to hit the ball, find it, hit it again, as quickly as possible, in the fewest number of strokes, until it finds the cup. Once called to the tee, the group is on the clock. So begins its obligation. Dawdling or late golfers can quickly back up play. Many are behind before a ball has even been struck.

All anyone can ask of a golfer, regardless of experience or skill, is to make an effort to keep up, play briskly, observe the game's manners, and show consideration for the course and others.

A round of golf begins and ends with a handshake. Golf is an individual pastime, but its pleasures and disappointments are shared. Pulling for one another comes easily. There are ultimately only two opponents: us and the course. If not exactly teammates for the next four hours golfers are together on something of a quest, sharing the game's highs and lows.

"Remember they were friends," wrote novelist P.G. Wodehouse. "For years they had shared each other's sorrows, joys, and golf balls, and sliced into the same bunkers."

FIRST-TEE INTRODUCTIONS

Teams might be paired up on the first tee or bets made. Be honest. "I'm just getting started," or "Usually around 55 for nine holes"; however you want to couch it, is fine. There's no reason to belittle or apologize. Others are just trying to get a sense of what's in store. No one knows what's going to happen. Should you come to establish a handicap, which numerically calculates skill level, simply announcing that you're a 21 or a 36 will suffice. (More on handicaps later.)

> "The hardest thing about golf is being on the tee with people watching you hit the ball if you're not a good player or just an average golfer."
> —Wayne Gretzky, *Edmonton Sun*, July 23, 2002

All golfers get nervous, and never more so than during the expectant moments on the first tee. For new golfers, the tension can be partially alleviated by addressing it. You might say: "Please share any tips you can to help me keep up. I've never played here before." Beware! The invitation is a double-edged sword. Every golfer setting foot on a course shares certain obligations that have nothing whatsoever to do with skill. *All golfers pledge to play in a timely manner, to respect the game and its traditions, to respect others, and to respect the golf course.* You're learning. Others can appreciate that. *What you are most definitely NOT asking for is swing tips.* Therein lies the danger.

PLEASE DON'T TELL US WHERE IT HURTS

For some golfers an airing of medical complaints amounts to a first-tee ritual. In few other circumstances are strangers so forthcoming with personal medical history. Newcomers may feel compelled to chime in with a variation of "I'm just terrible," or, "This is going to be awful. I'll hurt your game." Another familiar refrain, often heard from experienced golfers: "I haven't played in months / years / since . . ." Give them this much: they can be creative. You'd likely get a shorter answer checking on the health of an elderly aunt. Not only are these charlatans talking themselves out of what is supposed to be a pleasant experience, they're not exactly laying the groundwork for a fun-filled afternoon, that is—unless your idea of fun is listening to four hours of whining. Another old reliable centers on the condition of the lower back, but this can quickly veer into comparisons of mysterious tropical maladies, allergies, phantom pains, impending surgeries, and so on. Hypochondriacs and pessimists forget that each round is a blank canvas. Why not wait and see what happens? The experienced player shouldn't be burdened with listening to a broken record, nor should she have to be a crutch to a perfect stranger, continually reassuring a frail human psyche. *Golf is a game.* Likewise, the newcomer can hardly be expected to burst with empathy for the experienced golfer who, despite being plagued by dizzy spells, tendonitis, and a raging hangover, can only—ho-hum—manage another 73. Apologies are necessary only when someone gets beaned or otherwise contravenes the spirit and sportsmanship of golf. The relative merits of everyone's game will be apparent soon enough. There's a truism in golf that there's always someone better—and worse. Walk away from a hole with a seven, and half of the golfers could care less and the other half will wish it was an eight.

○ One of the PGA Tour's best liked to complain that his putting had gotten so bad, he "couldn't find water off a boat." The self-deprecating humor of golf is legendary, beloved and, especially in context, very funny. Try and take the embarrassing moments in stride.

TAKING YOUR MARK

Selecting the proper tees is a golfer's most important decision. Most courses offer several sets. Resort courses may have as many as five different sets of tees on every hole. These separate starting lines accommodate all skill levels. Choose wisely.

Tees, like ski slopes, are ranked by difficulty. The best skiers take the hardest trails; the best golfers typically select the most challenging route, the back tees. Beginning skiers stick to the easier trails; new golfers play the forward or regular tees. Golf makes allowances. From the right tees each player will be appropriately challenged.

Let's assume a beginning skier, to go along with the group, chooses to ski the expert slope. The results could be calamitous. No bones may be broken doing the equivalent in golf, but it's fair to say that the newcomer is in for a very long afternoon. Even if we were to ski the same mountain, but on different slopes, the experience wouldn't exactly be shared. Golf is different. It allows golfers to play the same course—though differently—together. Competitive golf also has a system of handicapping that further evens things out. *No golfer should feel obligated to play from one set of tees because others do so.* Make the appropriate call. There's no reason why two golfers, for instance, can't play from the forward tees and two from the championship tees. Let the better players do what's right for them. Make the proper selection, or ask the course officials for a recommendation. In the end, the correct choice will be better for everyone, increasing the odds of a pleasant round. Resorts now commonly step in, steering guests to the proper set. A beginning skier risks life and limb on the expert slopes. The ill-advised golfer will be similarly out of his element, risking psychological, if not physical, trauma. Golf is more fun from the proper tees.

BE MINDFUL

When golfers play off separate tees, better players will invariably reach the back tees first, and thus play first. Occasionally, they will forget that others have not yet hit and speed off in their cart. This is especially vexing when the sexes are paired. Women tee off from farther up, normally going last. On men's behalf, the forward tees may be slightly obscured, set off to the side. It happens. The slight is unintentional and should be handled gracefully, even humorously, by both the aggrieved and negligent parties. *Every golfer, not just those playing first or best, deserves equal consideration.*

DRAWING STRAWS

Flip a coin, a tee, draw straws—formalities should be kept to a minimum. Got a ball in your hand? A tee? The right club? Terrific. Step on up and hit. Please, none of this forced, unspoken, formality:

"After you."
"No, you first."
"Oh, I insist."
"But I couldn't."

To which we add: But you *must!* Should the invitation be extended to lead off, accept it. Should an opening present itself, seize it. If you're not ready, encourage someone else. Folks are waiting. This isn't butting in line. You're not changing sides, as in tennis, or taking a time-out. Or playing out of turn. The game is on. "I'm ready, I'll go," is appropriate and commendable. On every tee box, someone should immediately step up and play if the fairway ahead is open. Those still sorting themselves out should keep an eye on others. Mind that zipped pocket, dropped club, or trailing conversation during someone's swing. Have an extra ball and a few tees handy to save doubling back for provisions.

○ **Practice swings are not required and remain a lingering source of inertia, the golf equivalent of Chinese water torture. One should be enough. Be careful not to strike the turf and take a divot.**

HONOR

The first player has the *honor*. It has nothing to do with courage or valor, merely the order of play. No one in golf is ever denied a turn. On subsequent holes, the player with the lowest score plays first. When separate tees are involved, the players from the back tees generally play first. With two players on a tee, the one with the lowest score usually goes first.

Observing the honor can slow play. When the way is clear, golfers should be assertive in stepping up. Taking turns without delay keeps play moving. As soon as one player hits, the next player should immediately move into position.

READY GOLF

A salvo in the war against slow play, ready golf is a great way of making up time and keeping pace. Honor is dispensed with; so is pretense. Providing the way is clear, golfers fire when ready. A possible exception: the first tee or those occasions when everyone arrives on the tee more or less together *and* someone has just done something remarkable, say, scoring a birdie! Then a quick fuss can be made and the way cleared for the Honorable First Golfer.

YOUR ATTENTION, PLEASE

It behooves us to remain still, safely out of harm's way when others are playing a shot. No practice swings, ball washing, or jamming a club back in the bag. Curtail sudden movements. Innocence will not be excused. Among friends, the unsuspecting offense may go unchallenged; among strangers or serious golfers it could provoke an unsettling silence or rebuke. Stand still until the swing is completed.

Occasionally tee boxes aren't big enough to accommodate everyone, necessarily dictating where golfers stand. Generally, the best place to wait is alongside and even with the golfer, outside the tee markers defining the area of play. Alongside affords a good vantage point to watch the ball in flight. It also provides the golfer on the tee with the comfort of knowing that it's safe to play. Golfers have acute peripheral vision. Courtesy insists a vigilance regarding one's movements. Standing directly behind a golfer on the tee is discouraged, as it is on the fairway or on the green. Do not be surprised, or miffed, should someone ask you to move, even just a step this way or that. It's their prerogative. Golf needs no additional, even perceived, distractions. There's no penalty involved, but the Rules of Golf on this point are explicit: "No one should move, talk, or stand close to or directly behind the ball or the hole when a player is addressing the ball or making a stroke."

Creative and functional, if a tad excessive.

HAVING A BALL

Always know the make of ball you're playing. With dozens of golfers jockeying for position, balls going hither and yon, being able to say, "That's mine, a Blue Dot with a red mark over the B," saves time. It also suggests a golfer who is on top of things.

In formal competition, players individually mark their balls before the round, though few go as far as PGA Tour player Duffy Waldorf, who lets his kids go wild on his with various colored Sharpies.

Marking your ball is not only useful in identifying it. Playing a wrong ball is a costly penalty, two strokes in stroke play, loss of hole in match play. The ball must be replayed from the original location or the player risks disqualification.

RULES FOR THE TEEING GROUND

1. Tee up your ball between the two markers. Your feet don't have to be between the markers but the ball must be between or behind them.

2. Should you swing intending to hit the ball and miss—that counts one stroke. Should you inadvertently hit the ball during a practice swing, accidentally knocking it off the tee, it doesn't count. Retee the ball and start again with a clear con science. (No fair claiming a practice swing should you "whiff" trying to make contact.)

BEAUTIFUL! I MEAN . . . OH

Be sure before offering compliments. Golf balls are notoriously fickle, even malevolent. Especially with better playing strangers, defer comment for a few holes until a sense emerges of what for him or her is in fact a good shot. A fabulous shot to us may be, for a better player, less than satisfactory, merely OK, or even disappointing.

Closely follow errant shots. Helping someone find the ball speeds play and makes friends; it's one of those things golfers do for one another. Judging a ball's distance and direction can be difficult. It's truly aggravating how often shots barely off the tee can hide. Talk about embarrassing. Then there's having hit an apparently passable shot only to come up missing. Keep an eye on it. As a ball appears headed toward oblivion, try and line up the flight with a tree, a rock—something in the foreground—that will help narrow the search.

Responding to a less than stellar shot can be awkward. We defer to the exceptional insight of writer Pat Ward-Thomas: "When I hit a lousy shot, the last thing I want is condolences. The only suitable reaction is dead silence! Furthermore, the worst thing that anyone can say is, 'It's only a game.' The hell it's only a game!"

AN UNWELCOME GUEST

A mulligan is a "do-over," powerfully addictive, and an infernal source of slow play. Mulligans don't exist—officially—but every golfer has indulged. Some golfers mistakenly treat them as entitlements whenever they hit a bad tee shot, but they should never be automatic. Overdosing on mulligans will certainly annoy others as they contravene the very essence of golf etiquette—consideration of others and keeping up.

When taking one—and it's one and *only* one—be quick about it. As a courtesy, ask permission, since it is an imposition, unnecessarily delaying play. Mulligans are only permissible on uncrowded courses and when you are playing with close friends and relatives. (It pains us to commit even to this in print.) Occasionally, in charity tournaments, in the quest to raise more funds, mullys are sold as get-out-of-jail-free cards, good anywhere on the course.

Mulligans are another rite of passage, no more a part of the real, true game of golf than is "FBI" (first ball in) in championship tennis. Wherever the ball goes, that's where it's played. Mulligans make a mockery of the rules and the spirit of golf, and they are expressly forbidden in formal or competitive golf. Simply dropping another ball and hitting it, pretending the first shot never happened, is anathema to the game's virtues, justly frowned upon as taking the easy way out. In Scotland, where a fast pace of play is still the norm, they call mulligans "playing three off the tee." In other words, the concept of a freebie does not exist, an estimable expression of personal responsibility.

DRIVER'S ED

Carts are a convenience, but they are also a distraction, something else to be concerned with beyond the game. Those who would rather not drive a cart should alert the attendant to slide their bag to the passenger side or simply switch it out at the first opportunity. Accessories like the cart's Global Positioning System may require some hands-on activation, akin to setting up a computerized bowling score. If programming the VCR at home is problematic, it's best to have the attendant or cart partner activate it.

They may seem innocuous, but carts are vehicles, and as such they've ended up overturned in bunkers, lost over cliffs, and submerged in lakes. Fatal accidents are a grim reality. A sharp turn can easily throw a passenger. Branches can clip someone's face; feet can be run over. Then there's the cart brake, which clicks when properly set, one of the modern game's great annoyances. Incidentally, that hideous sound carts make backing up, cousin to the delivery truck beeping in reverse, should be kept to an absolute minimum. It doesn't exactly contribute to the ambiance of being outdoors. Try to avoid reverse, screeching tires, sharp turns, and abrupt starts and sudden stops that spill drinks and fray nerves.

VALET PARKING

Park alongside the first tee, never ahead of it. There will likely be a ball washer or a stone marker bearing a diagram of the hole, or a stairway leading up to the tee, something that says *here*. It might be a part of the cart path that extends closer to the tee, providing a passing lane. A cart's four wheels should remain on pavement.

Walkers pull up roughly to the same spot, making sure their bags won't be in anyone's way on the tee box.

CART PATHS ONLY

Golf courses are not (yet) defaced with traffic lights and signals, and carts don't (yet) come with brake lights, turn signals, or, God forbid, horns, but the few posted signs must be observed. One announcing Cart Paths Only insists that carts never leave the pavement. It's typically invoked when the course is wet and most susceptible to damage. This may not seem like a big deal, but consider the cumulative effect of days and weeks of half-ton vehicles driving across the tender turf.

When it's "CPO," golfers must pull the cart up even with their shots and walk out and back to their balls. (Hint: Take a few extra clubs to save a trip back.) The rule is routinely in force on all par threes, even in dry conditions. The cart must stay on the path.

Ninety degrees means straight out from the cart path
and straight back.

THE 90-DEGREE RULE

This rule permits golfers to drive out onto the fairway and back on a straight line, hence the name. Carts should return to the path after shots have been played. A common exception: When one player has not hit the ball very far, it's permissible to pull the cart up *along the rough* rather than go all the way back across the fairway, up twenty yards, say, and out again to reach the ball.

It may sound complicated, but the fact is carts add another layer; convenience comes at a cost. On foot we simply move to the ball as the crow flies. But such is the price of progress. *When a shot appears to require a 5-iron, grab both the 6- and 7-irons, or even the 8-iron or the 7-wood, just in case.* Save yourself a trip. Carts disrupt golf's natural rhythm, but they do make it easier for golfers who otherwise couldn't enjoy the game, not to mention saving time doubling back for a dropped headcover or lost club.

The absence of any signs does not mean anything goes. Wet spots, low spots, puddles, overhanging limbs, and roped-off areas should be scrupulously avoided. Stewardship of the golf course most assuredly includes driving responsibly. A cart should never be on the golf course within seventy yards of the green. Return to the path.

HOP IN

Carts are not blameless with respect to slow play. Save time by hopping back in the cart after a shot rather than returning the club directly to the bag. Wait until the cart next stops. Kill two birds with one stone. Do this rather than searching for the headcover, finding it, placing it back on the club, placing the club back in the right slot, jiggling it so it goes all the way in, sitting down—and, finally, pulling off.

Carts will be covered again in the fairway and around the green. For the moment, sit back, enjoy the ride. We'll close by politely asking smokers to treat their fellow passengers with the courtesy they'd extend in sharing a cab or table.

CIGARS AND CIGARETTES

Golf courses, you'll notice, are littered with butts. It has even been suggested that fairways have become so befouled by cigars, which frankly can look like something the dog left behind, to merit a notation in the rules as loose impediments. Every tee has a trash receptacle. These are not to be confused with the buckets of sand meant to refill divots on par-three tee boxes. They are not ashtrays.

DEAR ARNOLD

Golfers often compare notes about the club used on various shots. This is another regular feature of casual golf, not as bad as indiscriminate mulligans, but not considered cricket as far as the rules are concerned. When golfers are playing "real" golf, in a competition: keeping score, observing the rules, playing the ball "down," golfers are not allowed to ask each other for advice. Asking another player, "What did you hit?" that is, consulting with one another over what club was used for a particular shot, is construed as soliciting advice.

On par-three holes, for instance, the correct club selection is a riddle that changes with the breeze, the circumstances, and individual preference. The right choice can make all the difference. Players can peek into each other's bags, but just so you know there are situations, and for some golfers this will be always be the case, that asking "What'd ya hit?" is considered bad form. You will also encounter golfers who play golf with friends but don't necessarily play friendly golf. They play seriously, competitively, and fairly. These golfers would never ask until after all shots have been played, when asking is allowed, although they're not above checking a bag to see which club is missing.

BRIEFING

• A round of golf should begin and end with a handshake.

• Advice can be lethal. If it will help you maintain your pace, or learn the nuances of etiquette, terrific. If it plunges you into the depths of new-golfer swing-advice be firm. Insist it wait until after the round. Bite your tongue should the words "What am I doing wrong?" form on your lips.

• Pull the cart up even with the tee. Invariably, there will be an area akin to a parking space. Typically, this area is near stairs or a path leading directly to the tee. Or look for a ball washer or relief of the hole.

• Stand even with a swinging golfer, in view. Avoid standing directly behind a golfer anywhere on the golf course. Don't be surprised if someone takes exception. Give yourself and others enough room to safely take practice swings. When a golfer puts his tee into the ground, hold your position.

• One needn't apologize for, explain, or preface bad (or good) shots with an exhaustive litany of medical ailments. Good and bad shots speak for themselves.

• Play the right tees. Do it for yourself. Do it for others. Do it for the golfers teeing off an hour from now. You needn't feel you have to defer to better players. To golf's eternal benefit, the game can be shared among different skill levels.

• Drive carts sensibly. Respect the fragility of the golf course and the human body. A convenience, carts present an additional set of etiquette issues. Observe all signs and policies. Carts don't have brake lights, turn signals, or, thank God, horns.

• Carts, just like golfers, should ideally be positioned alongside, never directly behind, in view, but out of the way; never close enough that a golfer has to wonder about his backswing.

• Obey the signs, avoid wet areas, respect the ropes. Never drive near a green. Be cognizant of the cart brake and the noisy intrusion of backing up. Carts can skid, get involved in head-ons, and roll off cliffs and into lakes.

• Be certain a good shot is a good shot before offering compliments.

• Mulligans are a blight on the civility, pace, virtue, and high ethical standards of golf. Should you fall into temptation, be quick about it. Always carry an extra ball in the event of mishaps.

• Closely watch tee shots. On the way to your ball, help others locate theirs.

> "Provided there is a clear hole ahead of you, you must not clog the course if the match following you is waiting to go through, but beckon them to play through. Do the same in the event of a lost ball." —*Golf Penalties and Etiquette* (1904)

Quietly bring everything to a halt. Be ready to play when it's your turn.

5 ON THE FAIRWAY

"Move smartly between shots and be ready
to play your shot when it is your turn."
—Scorecard from Lahinch Golf Club, Co. Clare, Ireland

Golf is a game of turn taking. From the first tee shot until the
last putt drops, it is always someone's turn. Two people never
play at once, but the order never stops. Someone is always
away. Timely play and safety insist that everyone know and
agree upon whose turn it is. The Rules of Golf dictate protocol in formal competition; in recreational play someone may
suggest hitting out of order by saying, "After you," or "I'm
ready, I'll go." Each golfer has the responsibility to play expediently. The only exception is when others might be in danger
of being struck by a ball. Then it's best to hold off.

GETTING THERE

Research proves walking is no slower than riding. Either way,
golf should be played *efficiently*. Before golfers rode, they got
some exercise. They moved directly to their balls, fell into a
gentle rhythm, and never had to grit their teeth over a
screeched cart brake. They could hold a conversation taking

in the beauty of the landscape, silently studying their next shot as they walked. Our nation is tragically overweight and underexercised. Golf may not be a vigorous aerobic workout, but walking burns more calories than riding, and it's cheaper. A 9-hole course typically spans two or three miles; an 18-hole course covers about five miles. True, many courses no longer permit walking. Those built expressly for carts, even if walking were permitted, would challenge a triathlete. It's unfortunate. But walking is making a comeback.

There's no mystery why carts are so ubiquitous. They make money. Their use has been a Faustian bargain. Golf is a better game played on foot and the positive physical effects are irrefutable. Not convinced? Well, then, when was the last time you heard someone come off the 18th hole raving about the cart?

STAGE CUES

When a golfer prepares to play (in golfspeak: addresses) a shot, quietly bring everything to a stop. Preferably stand even with—not in front of and not behind—the person playing. Remain outside the golfer's peripheral vision. The same goes for the cart. It's impolite to stand, or pull up, directly behind a golfer. There is a tendency for some golfers to stop and watch out of an exaggerated sense of politeness. When someone gets set to play, veer off to the side, be mindful of your position. Stand still during the swing. Once the ball has gone, the light has changed. Follow the ball's flight on your way.

○ Particularly with carts, steer clear of fairway soft and wet spots.

START IT UP

The golfer farthest from the green is deemed "away," and plays first. It's long been thought that the saddest words in golf are a variation of "It's still your turn," meaning "You're still away." Ideally, we would all play well enough that the rotation of play continues in order until we reach the green, but there are times when one player may hit one or more shots before relinquishing his turn. Should you be ready to play (but not be officially away), in the quest of saving time, seize the opportunity. In recreational play, when it's convenient, honor should be observed. When it's not officially your turn, but there's an opening, a simple, courteous "I'm ready. I'll go ahead" should suffice. In recreational play there's no penalty for hitting out of turn. Tournament golf is another matter, which we'll cover in time.

NOW?

Have at it with the way clear. With two players equidistant, the ritual dance of "after you" should be abbreviated. Is the other player, across the fairway, plucking blades of grass and throwing them up in the air, clearly not ready? That's your cue. Is he looking at you for a sign? If you're ready, go ahead. Occasionally, better golfers will choose to wait, say, in the fairway on a par 5 until the green ahead has cleared before attempting the demanding shot. They wait to avoid possibly hitting into the group on the green, even if they're 200 yards or more away. That's fine. They can wait. It may, however, be safe for you to play. OK, you're thinking, but it's not my shot. I don't want to be impolite. How to handle it? Offer to go ahead and *play up* rather than observing the farthest-out-plays-first rotation. The sooner everyone hits, the better for everyone—and likely the better the shot.

IN THE PUBLIC INTEREST

How long does it take to hit a golf ball? Three seconds? Less? Still, listen closely and you can almost hear the gears and rotors grinding as golfers take aim. Could rigor mortis be setting in? Tension remains the golf swing's worst enemy. The longer we wait, the harder it is to hit a good shot. Anxiety works its way up from the hands to the central nervous system and back, leaving rivulets of stress from the shoulders through the forearms, wrists, and fingers, all whittling away at confidence. It's long been a truism that the longer one has to think over a shot, the worse the result. Unquestionably, there's a point of diminishing returns, which recalls an old saying: Miss 'em quick.

The legendary Bobby Jones believed, as with most things, that the first impression on a golf shot was more often than not the best. Swing away before the tension has a chance to worm its way into full-blown paralysis.

There's plenty of blame on this point to go around. Golfers are not often taught the Big Picture along with the golf swing. Time is not an issue on the practice tee. Nor, to the extent that it is on the golf course, is etiquette. Emphasis is rarely placed on helping newcomers adjust to the grander, exponentially more complex, situations encountered out on the course. *The new golfer is taught the mechanics of the golf swing but not the consequences of taking too long to make it.* The novice golfer deserves some slack. Television hasn't helped. The pros provide an unrealistic benchmark for weekend golfers—they can be very slow—but then their careers are on the line. Still, they also struggle against the effects of inertia. One would think that this would provide sufficient motivation to keep things moving, but unless golfers recognize the problem and take the initiative to play faster, the game will continue at a snail's pace.

Novelist John Updike exquisitely captured the malaise in his short story "Drinking from a Cup Made Cinchy (After Reading Too Many Books on How to Play Golf)." It includes an appendix of all too accurate "Helpful Hints." They're indicative of the blizzard of thoughts that confound the mind. He mentions three:

1. Don't be tense.
2. Don't be "loose."
3. Think of yourself not as an assembly of hinged joints inflexibly connected by rods of calcium but as a plastic, pliant animal, capable of warmth, wit, and aspiration.

CRUISING SPEED

What does maintaining pace mean? A group is doing so when it is playing in the time allotted to it. Some groups play faster, some slower. Some golfers understand hurry, others don't know the meaning of the word. Some holes are harder than others and necessarily take longer to complete.

The first group off in the morning, unimpeded, may finish forty-five minutes faster than the group behind them even though they started eight minutes apart. Try and keep the group ahead in your sights, close enough to be waiting on them. Arriving at a par 3, ideally, the group ahead is putting out. Faster groups can be let through at this point, but if your group is doing its best against the clock, you're holding your own. As Tom Barber, head golf professional at Griffith Park in Los Angeles, puts it: *A group's position is behind the group in front NOT in front of the group behind.*

○ Just because no one's pushing your group doesn't mean you're keeping pace. If you're not waiting on the group in front, you're playing too slow.

When you miss a shot, really mishit it—it goes a couple of feet—step up, start fresh, and hit it again. The world becomes hazy, and remorse mingles with embarrassment and pride. Whatever, be assured your companions only want to see one thing: the next shot. Nothing need be said. No hands on hips. No melodramatic displays or tortured explanations. Just hit the ball. Experienced players are often guilty of taking too long. Don't be misled into thinking slow play is a beginner's problem. Far from it. Instruction books, magazines, videos, and TV commentators all stress the importance of a routine before every golf shot, a methodical waltz that may include grip check, stance check, target check, a waggle or two, deep breath, another target check, practice swing, and so on. All this for an action that takes a blink of an eye. The premise is sound, but some *pre-shot routines* merely prolong the inevitable. Etiquette insists they be brief.

Electronic sensors now routinely track the movement of carts around the golf course, cueing management to the pace-of-play trouble spots. The technological sophistication also provides distance yardages so golfers won't have to search for yardage markers in the fairway. They're meant to save time.

○ PGA Tour players officially have forty seconds to play each shot when it is their turn. They get an extra twenty seconds when they are first to hit into a par 3, first to hit approach shots, and first to play around or on the greens.

REHEARSAL

One practice swing is enough. Three people are awaiting their turns, and very soon four others will come up from behind. A practice swing is for loosening up, alerting others that the wait is over and a shot imminent. Separated by the width of the fairway, backs turned to one another, practice swings can be safely and discreetly taken at will.

TAXI!

Golfers routinely mistake carts for taxicabs. In many situations it will be faster for one player to get out, take a few clubs (in the event of a change of heart), and hoof it to the ball. Perhaps the cart can be parked halfway. Perhaps the passenger can drop off the driver instead of being chauffeured. Offer to get out and walk. Bottom line: What's fastest? Whatever will accomplish both shots as quickly as possible is best.

PLAYING THROUGH

Never, it is written, has so much hostility been shown toward a group known simply as "in front." Playing through—letting another group pass—is one of those moments in a round where etiquette, common sense, and diplomacy converge. It can contain elements of road rage, but golf was never meant as a race. There's no disgrace in letting a group play through *when circumstances dictate*. It's the proper thing to do.

When should a group play through? It's something like interpreting a traffic jam. If there's nowhere to go, the accident not yet cleared ahead, moving up a car length or two is not going to make any difference. So it is on a crowded golf course. *When your group is keeping pace, routinely waiting to play, you have reason to feel aggrieved should another group insist on playing through*. Remember, what's happening behind is not the measure of a group's pace.

When your group has lost ground, however, and, despite everyone's best efforts, a hole has opened up ahead (no one is on the fairway or the green of the next hole), as a courtesy the faster group should be offered the opportunity to pass. They may not take it, but they should be invited to do so.

○ Did we mention that a group's position on the course is behind the group in front, *not* in front of the group behind?

Playing through is not like passing on the freeway, jockeying for position and seizing an opening. It is a favor requested and politely granted. It commonly takes place on par-3 holes because these holes are shorter and played faster. Theoretically, it's easier here to accomplish the transition. For the group giving ground, the best place to let faster golfers through is with everyone together on the tee or on the green. There are times—everyone in the rough, say—when golfers can merely step aside, wave others on, and resume searching for their drives. Mission accomplished.

A group that is prepared to step aside may, on par threes, hit their initial tee shots and then vacate the tee. Another convenient place to let groups through is at the "turn," the end of the first nine holes. While the lead group is visiting the snack bar, the "hares" can pass after being waved on or first asking permission.

THOSE PLAYING THROUGH

- Should skip mulligans.
- Should never fire warning shots into slower groups to *get them moving*.
- Should do so briskly.
- Should be gracious and thank those letting them pass.
- Should not consider it a birthright. Better players cannot assume the privilege if the group ahead is keeping pace.

THOSE BEING PLAYED THROUGH

- Should take the opportunity to converse, discuss last week's pro tour highlights, enjoy their surroundings, or indulge in a practice swing-a-thon.
- Should make themselves as unobtrusive as possible for the sake of safety and decorum while others hit their shots.
- Should not restart play until the passing group is safely out of range.

Playing through should be a last resort. *The far preferable solution is for the offending group to speed up.* Sometimes that's impossible, say, when two people in the group can't find their balls. Letting people through can slow things down. It's like the one slow car on the expressway. If everyone has to pass, it takes more time. Better the slow car should speed up. Play ready golf, forego the beverage cart, do whatever it takes to maintain the position originally assigned to the group when the round began.

The last word on what admittedly can be a hornet's nest, not helped by prospective disputing parties bearing clubs, goes to Judith Martin, the inimitable *Miss Manners*. She writes appropriately for us, though on an unrelated matter: "Etiquette has ways of settling things that are less fun but more effective. Its policy, like that of any sensible government, is to try diplomacy before declaring war."

○ **FORE!** should be shouted long and lustily *any* time it appears a golfer may be in danger of being struck by a ball. Whether it's your shot or not hardly matters; even if you're not sure the ball will reach them, you're obligated to sound the alarm. The golfers watching may have a better read on where it's headed than the golfer who hit it. Shout it out. It's the least that can be done.

GRIDLOCK

Maintaining a good pace is more fun, better exercise, better for one's game, the right thing to do, all that good stuff. No golfer thinks he's slow. It's *always* someone else. Some golfers don't know any better because they've never been taught otherwise. That's not an excuse, just an unfortunate fact of modern golfing life.

Dean Knuth, former senior director of the USGA's handicapping department, has studied slow play. In his interviews, *deliberate* golfers invariably get defensive. They say things like "I've never been told that I am slow," and "I don't believe it," or they get indignant: "I paid good money to enjoy this round, and I deserve to take as much time as I need." Harrumph.

○ **For more on slow play, check out Knuth's research at www.popeofslope.com.**

Newcomers and women are often unfairly singled out for slow play—as if speed of play and consideration for others were solely predicated on skill or gender. If that were true, the very best golfers in the world would be the fastest, and that's not the case. The slowest golfers would then be the least skilled, and that's not true, either.

Ultimately, pace of play boils down to attitude. It requires consideration, organization, effort, and tact. The *turtles* selfishly spoil golf for those behind them.

A slow-playing group is akin to a traffic accident—with rubbernecking delays, road rage, frayed nerves—everything but a traffic copter doing the updates. Play is altered long after the debris has been cleared.

Golf is slower today, no question about it, and it's slower in the United States than it is anywhere else. The PGA Tour routinely endures five-hour rounds playing as twosomes and threesomes. It has led to considerable hand-wringing and, on rare occasions, fines. There's an increasing awareness that something needs to be done at the professional level for the good of the game, at the very least to set a better example.

Scottish caddies may be the last line of defense. Golf is played so much faster across the Atlantic. The story is told of the caddy assigned to a *very* slow group. The round dragged on until he couldn't stand it.

"Can ye not speed u' th' pace?" he pleaded. "I'm losing me will t' live."

Some years ago, pro golf officials singled out one promising player for his slow play. "I had to learn what hurt me in the long run and what bothered other players, and I had to learn to make my own adjustments," he later recalled. "I was behind on every hole and forcing my fellow competitors to rush, and it wasn't fair. I was hurting them and had to change the way I played." And so Jack Nicklaus, a great golfer and sportsman, did.

A MATTER OF TIMING

Let's say we're playing as a foursome, golf's standard unit of measure. By Dean Knuth's calculations, a typical par 4 should take about 12 minutes to play, a par 5 about 18 minutes, a par 3 about 9 minutes. Each player in our imaginary foursome wastes 15 seconds a hole. How hardly matters. Fifteen seconds doesn't seem that appalling, but multiplied by the four members of the group, a slow round starts to take shape. A minute is added to the length of the round for one hole. (4 players × 15 seconds = 60 seconds, or 1 minute.) Now multiply that by 18 holes, and the group is already behind its recommended pace by 18 minutes.

HOWDY SHERIFF

When diplomacy fails, call for reinforcements. Their name conveys some legal standing or at least a hint of Old West authority: rangers, marshals, player assistants, course ambassadors. The eyes and ears of the pro shop, their role is to help keep the peace and the pace.

These brave men and women—often working for little more than occasional free golf and range privileges—are officialdom's first line of defense against slow play. For anything from a lost pitching wedge to a flat tire to cardiac arrest, the marshals are a welcome presence. They take on a thankless task because they enjoy being around the game.

○ **Strange-but-true marshal tales: A ranger approaches a slow group. "You've fallen two holes behind the group in front," he tells them. Responds a golfer: "The green fee's good for all day." "Yes," says the marshal, "but that doesn't mean it should take all day."**

It may appear that marshals are merely driving around the golf course, but they're actually timing every group. They know where the problems are. They know how long it takes each group. They return lost clubs, deliver messages. These are the people to go to when anything's seriously amiss.

PICKING UP

Picking up means one of two things. First, on encountering a ball anywhere on the golf course, never lift it. Closely examine it on the ground, cautiously turn it just enough to read the label or look for a mark. Ideally, a golf ball should not be lifted from the time it's placed on a tee until it reaches the green (where it can be marked and cleaned). If the ball is truly lost, it's yours, finders-keepers. *But*, if not, expect to hear about it from the owner; best to leave it alone unless you're absolutely, positively certain. Then, and only then, are you welcome to it. New club technology has produced prodigious distance, if not prodigious accuracy. Be forewarned that the ball seemingly lost may only be recently orphaned. (Here again, knowing which ball you're playing will come in handy.)

Searching for lost balls can be addictive. There are those who can't resist the opportunity. Perhaps one day a cure will be found.

Picking up is also a new golfer's out. When you've had enough, when you've played the hole and come up short, when others are waiting, not just waiting but staring at their watches, pocket the ball and move on. Live to fight another hole. If things are just not working, try again on the green or on the next tee. The new recreational golfer is accorded certain liberties in maintaining a good pace and learning the game. This is one of them. Established golfers will appreciate this gracious gesture on behalf of the greater good. You will return.

COVERING YOUR TRACKS

Good and bad shots produce divots, the golf term for a tear in the ground from a swing. They are an accepted part of the game except on practice swings. Etiquette asks that they always be repaired, for maintenance reasons as well as sportsmanship and aesthetics. They're no fun to play out of, a definite and often preventable disadvantage to the golfer who finds her ball has rolled into one. Replacing divots allows the earth to put down new roots. Simply return it as if it were a puzzle piece. Firmly step it in place. This will keep it from being pulled back out by mowers. Untended divots can leave turf susceptible to disease or weed infestation. Such negligence necessitates the attention of the superintendent and his staff and takes up time better spent elsewhere. Divots are on-course litter and should not be blithely ignored.

On some courses, instead of replacing divots, containers or buckets are attached to carts and filled with sand or seed for repairing divots. This is often the case on courses in southern climates. Walking to your ball, take one of the containers along. There comes a point in each fairway, closing in on the green, where carts are no longer permitted passage and must return to the path. This area—fifty or sixty yards from the green—is where wedges are typically used, iron clubs with more loft, that take deeper divots. It takes only a moment to fix a few untended scars.

UCLA's golf team plays tony Bel-Air Country Club—a nifty perk—but not without observing the importance of golfers taking responsibility for course maintenance. In exchange for playing privileges, Bruin golfers are required to tow along buckets of sand, filling six divots on every hole. On the green they each have to repair four neglected pitch marks.

The Golf Course Superintendent's Association recommends divots be manually replaced unless there is a container of fill provided. If that's the case, use it. (Sometimes containers are attached to carts.) Anyone connected with the course can quell any confusion about which method is preferred.

○ **Always pick up a stray club. Hand it off to a marshal or drop it at the pro shop.**

ODOMETER CHECK

Take note of the distance markers posted in the fairway. Sprinkler head plaques denote the distance from the fairway to the green. They might be listed this way:

125
145
165

That means it's 125 yards from the sprinkler head to the front of the green, 145 yards to the center of the green, and 165

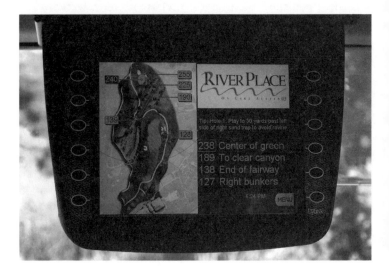

yards to the back of the green. Now locate which portion of the green the pin is set in and you have an idea of how long a shot is required. Golfers in the rough appreciate being given a yardage, which is entirely within the rules. On the way to your ball help out partners by finding and passing on the yardage.

Global Positioning Systems (GPS). Literally satellite-based, the cart screen will provide exact yardages.

Pin sheets. Sometimes a sheet is posted or provided in the cart in lieu of an on-board computer. It's a diagram of each green with numbers indicating the day's precise hole location in feet from the front and side edges of the green.

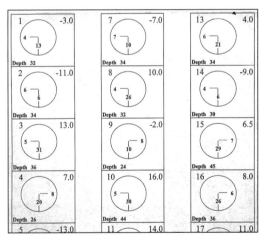

Better players will benefit from knowing exactly where the pin is located on the green. This pin sheet posts the number in the upper left corner as the hole (1–18). The number in the upper right corner shows precisely where the hole is located on that day, farther back or closer in feet.

Flag colors. The flag commonly offers a clue to the pin position, where the cup is literally "cut" into the ground. (Pin positions are often changed daily.) The scorecard will provide the key. All blue flags may mean a back pin position; all red flags for a front location.

Ball on Flagstick. When the flags are all the same color, there may be a small ball attached to the staff that tips the golfer to the day's hole location. With the ball set just under the flag, a back pin position is indicated. With the ball set halfway down the pole, it means the pin is cut in the center of the green. It follows then that the ball hanging toward the bottom signifies a front pin position.

All this is worth considering because greens can be as long as sixty or seventy yards. Regardless of the system in place, only golfers who know precisely how far they hit each club can benefit from all this information. For the newcomer a general idea of front, middle, back, right, or left pin position is sufficient.

FRONT

MIDDLE

BACK

DON'T ASK, DON'T TELL

The best advice we can give is to ignore it. Advice is a blight, and there's nothing more unpleasant than playing golf with someone giving instruction to someone else. Most of it, offered with the best of intentions, is worth exactly what it costs. The place to go over swing tips is on the driving range or over a cold one after the game in the 19th hole.

Couples can be the worst, although they have an undeniably humorous component. Barbara was once playing with her husband, Roane, a fine player. He put his tee shot in the water. So, too, it happened, did Barbara. "How could you do that?" Roane barked. "Good grief! You saw me go in the water. Why did you?" Be polite. Be solicitous. Be appreciative of another golfer's consideration, but be firm. Postpone advice to the appropriate time and place (after the round, on the range).

BRIEFING

• Don't believe for an instant that slow play is a beginner's problem, or a women's problem, or a junior's problem. It has less to do with skill than attitude. The best players in the world are some of the slowest.

• Why play fast? You'll play better golf. Keeping pace allows less time to think and brood, less time to waste, and the ability to keep moving and establish a rhythm.

• One practice swing is enough when the game is on. Avoid taking a divot on a practice swing. Your best opportunity to hit your best shot is made without delay.

• Nothing so easily prevented is more debilitating to course conditions or morale over time than neglected divots. Replacing them is a cornerstone of proper etiquette.

• Help others find their balls, determine yardage. Let them know when it's safe to play.

• Playing through is a privilege not a right. A group maintaining its pace (keeping up with the group in front) is under no obligation to let others play through. Playing through is best accomplished with a group together, on the green or the tee. Give ground willingly. If there's a problem, find a course marshal.

• Pick up when the hole has lost its appeal, and others are waiting.

• Before helping yourself to a lost ball, make sure it is in fact abandoned, not orphaned. Never pick up a ball unless you are certain.

> "The game of golf is in a fair way of becoming unplayable in America on account of the amazing and unconscionable slowness of American players. The prevalent idea that the American is a born hustler is sadly belied on the golf links. It may be that just because he has learned to travel in express subway trains the American has forgotten how to walk. On the golf links he walks terribly slowly."
> —H. J. Whigham, *The Common Sense of Golf* (1910)

A club must not be *grounded* in a hazard.

6 IN A WATER, SAND, OR LATERAL HAZARD

"The word *hazard* of course implies risk and that is as it should be. Hazards should be 'potential,' not certain, destinations. Some will strike fear into our hearts, but these are not necessarily the greatest assets of a course. It is the more subtle hazards you remember, those that lure you on to laugh at your own shortcomings."
—Peter Thomson, in the afterword to *Hazards* by Aleck Bauer

Much maligned, hazards give a course its definition and character. A prominent golf course architect suggests they are not fully appreciated for their role as lighthouses, guiding savvy golfers safely from trouble. They make the game interesting, challenging, and rewarding. Hazards most of all make us think.

They also require an awareness of decorum. Amusing as it may be when someone's ball lands in one, there is no need to comment. Feigned indifference is best.

DIGGING IN

A club may not be "grounded" (touch the ground) in a hazard. All the water, sand, and stones can be splattered and splashed in playing the actual shot from any hazard, but the club must not touch the water (or ground or sand) beforehand. Nothing can be disturbed on practice swings in a hazard, for good reason. Thrashing away in sand bunkers or other hazards would surely ruin them. That's why in taking a practice swing in a bunker the club must never touch the sand.

A DAY AT THE BEACH

The most common hazards are sand bunkers. Always enter and exit them from the low side. Resist the temptation to leap in from the high side or climb out over the top. Avoid treading on fragile slopes and overhangs.

TIDYING UP

When you're done, make the bunker presentable, just as considerate hikers "leave no trace behind" before breaking camp. The next hapless victim deserves a fair chance at recovery. A rake should be nearby, sometimes placed on the backs of carts or beside the *trap*, as a bunker is informally called. There is debate over where a rake should ideally be placed. The official consensus is alongside the bunker, not inside it.

INCOMING!

Players in hazards deserve a wide berth. No one knows how the ball will emerge. A golfer concentrating on a difficult shot has enough to worry about. Others should be alert to what may be coming and move aside, also making sure bags are far enough away so as not to interfere with an errant shot. A quick "heads up" may be in order.

Enter and exit a sand bunker from the low side.

LATERAL H$_2$O HAZARDS

Marked by red stakes or lines, *lateral* hazards are not quite as punitive as out of bounds (see chapter 9). When a ball finds its way into a lateral hazard, one does not have to return to replay the shot. The key difference between lateral water hazards and other hazards is location. A lateral hazard usually parallels the fairway. For the cost of one stroke, a new ball may be dropped within two club lengths from where the original shot entered the hazard (officially, where it *crossed the margin* of the hazard). That's one for the shot into the hazard, two for the penalty—drop alongside—playing three. You may also play it from inside the hazard, if you dare. Just remember not to ground your club. Or you can always play over from the original location. There are actually five options.

SPLISH, SPLASH

Marked by yellow stakes or lines, a water hazard does not have to be filled with water. It may be a drainage ditch or a dry creek bed. To determine where to *take a drop* (where to put a new ball into play), keep the hazard on a line between you and the hole. The rules insist that the only way across the hazard is to hit over it. Dropping alongside in this instance, as one would with a lateral, is not permitted.

Another option is to go back as far as desirable (sometimes this is an advantage), keeping the point where the ball originally entered the hazard between you and the hole. Same deal in counting when taking a drop: one in the water, two for the penalty, now playing three.

DROPPING IN

Stand erect, hold the ball at shoulder height and arm's length, drop it. If it rolls into the hazard twice (or rolls toward the hole, or more than two club lengths), you are permitted to redrop it and place the ball where it landed.

ENVIRONMENTAL HAZARDS

To spare golfers from traipsing through wildlife habitat, or sinking in mud up to their knees, blue stakes or lines denote areas they are forbidden to enter. Not for a ball. Not to take a closer look at a newborn fawn. Typically, a free drop is permitted to mollify golfers and keep them from being too adventurous.

TWO BALLS IN A BUNKER

When more than one player hits into the same bunker, some confusion is inevitable. With balls partially buried, it's entirely possible that a case of mistaken identity can occur and a wrong ball be played.

There's no penalty for playing a wrong ball out of a hazard. Go ahead and swing away. A ball may also be examined with the care of a paleontologist brushing off dust from dinosaur bones. If a mistake occurs, the owner whose ball has been accidentally played should drop a new ball on the same spot after recreating the lie. Play on. For a ball completely buried—before the mistaken identity occurred—it should be so again.

WHO'S AWAY?

The player in a bunker cannot assume he has the right-of-way to play first. It depends, as it does everywhere else after leaving the tee, on who is farthest from the hole. The person farthest away has the honor, be it from the fairway, in a bunker, or on the green.

LAST RESORT

When all else fails, there is always the hand *mashie*. Pick up the ball and toss it onto the green. In tournament play, this would never do; one would have to declare an unplayable lie or whack away until the ball is finally free, however many blows it takes. In recreational play, the newcomer can—after three or four unsuccessful attempts (each made quickly and decisively)—in the interests of time and sanity, pick up the ball or help it onto the green. Embarrassing? Perhaps, but opportunities for redemption are as near as the next shot.

LOOSE IMPEDIMENTS

One other essential hazard rule: Loose impediments may not be lifted or touched. Should twigs, grass clippings, leaves, or other natural objects find their way into a bunker, there they shall remain. No landscaping is permitted before playing a recovery shot. Obstructions—manmade objects such as cans, bottles, clubs, or the rake, if they've been left inside—may be lifted. It is not uncommon to come upon a ball partially submerged in a pool of collected rainwater in a sand bunker in need of repair. Under these circumstances, the ball may be moved, without penalty, to a dry area inside the bunker. The ball cannot be removed from the bunker or dropped closer to the hole.

> "The difference between a sand trap and water is the difference between a car crash and an airplane crash. You have a chance of recovering from a car crash."
>
> —Bobby Jones, *Bobby Jones on Golf*

A HAZARDOUS TALE

Jack, an experienced golfer, was taking his friend Sally out for her very first time on a golf course. To her pleasant surprise, Sally hit a nice drive off the first tee. After landing in the fairway, the ball took a funny hop and rolled into some leaves and small twigs on the edge of the fairway. Surveying her ball Sally wore a look of concern.

"You can pick up those sticks and leaves, if they're in your way," Jack called out. "Great," said Sally. "I wasn't sure you could lift anything around the ball."

After clearing away the impediments, she chose a 7-iron. Another solid hit. The ball came to rest just inside a bunker by the green. As she was about to play, Sally spied some twigs around her ball. She bent down to clear them away when Jack, keeping a close eye on things, shouted out:

"Wait! You can't do that. It's against the rules. You can't touch anything in the sand."

"Oh," said Sally, thinking back to the fairway. "I thought . . . Never mind."

She carefully avoided the twigs and played on as best she could. Out in one! The ball raced toward the flag, stopping on the green about twenty feet or so from the hole. "Nicely done," said Jack.

After dutifully raking the bunker, Sally was first to putt. Getting ready, sure enough, there were some leaves on the green in the path of her ball. "Hmmm," she thought, "I could move them on the fairway, but I couldn't move anything in a bunker. Now what?"

Jack, sensing her indecision, came once again to her aid. "You can pick up those leaves," he said, "or anything else on the green, for that matter, that's not attached."

"But you said . . ."

That's where we have to leave our two friends. It's the end of the story, if not the confusion. The moral is that there are three sections of the golf course, and as Sally discovered, different rules are in effect depending upon which section of the course a ball lands. *Through the green* means everywhere on the golf course *except* on the green and in hazards. Rules change in hazards, and they also change on the green. (PS: Not to worry. Sally collected herself and two-putted for an outstanding par.)

BRIEFING

- Always enter and exit bunkers from the low side.
- Remember not to *ground* a club in a hazard, including sand bunkers. Only hit the ground (water, sand) in playing your shot, not on practice swings.
- Being in a bunker doesn't necessarily mean one's away and can play first.
- After two or three tries at extricating your ball, pick up.

"If your adversary is badly bunkered, there is no rule against your standing over him and counting his strokes aloud, with increasing gusto as their number mounts up; but it will be a wise precaution to arm yourself with the niblick before doing so, so as to meet him on equal terms."

—Horace Hutchinson (1896)

7 ON THE GREEN

"Players who have holed out should not try
their putts over again when other players
are following them."   —Jack Burke, *Ten Lessons in Golf* (1921)

The baize on golf's billiard table, greens, are the most expensive part of the golf course to construct and maintain. Drive a cart across one, and the staff will take it personally. Scuffling feet, running, jumping, digging in, anything that mars the putting surface should be scrupulously avoided. Golfers play an active role in keeping the course in shape. Nowhere is this more evident than on the green, where etiquette transgressions are also magnified.

PARALLEL PARKING

Approaching the green there will be an area to the side meant for carts, similar to the teeing ground, perhaps an extended shoulder along the path. This provides a place to park and a natural pedestrian entrance and exit. *Before getting out to putt, drive the cart all the way around the green toward the next tee.* This smoothes the transition and saves golfers from having to double back. Bags and pull carts should likewise be carried or rolled around to the far side to afford a seamless exit.

Signs or ropes will direct carts back to the path at about one hundred yards from the green. Those unfamiliar with the course should locate the next tee or follow suit by placing their bags alongside those who know their way. It's a simple act, and it just takes a moment, but pulling the cart around or walking over and depositing the bag on the right side saves time.

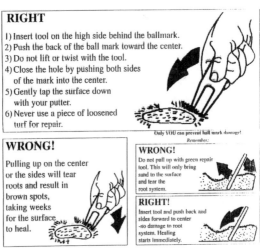

RIGHT

1) Insert tool on the high side behind the ballmark.
2) Push the back of the ball mark toward the center.
3) Do not lift or twist with the tool.
4) Close the hole by pushing both sides of the mark into the center.
5) Gently tap the surface down with your putter.
6) Never use a piece of loosened turf for repair.

Only YOU can prevent ball mark damage!

Remember:

WRONG!

Pulling up on the center or the sides will tear roots and result in brown spots, taking weeks for the surface to heal.

WRONG!

Do not pull up with green repair tool. This will only bring sand to the surface and tear the root system.

RIGHT!

Insert tool and push back and sides forward to center -no damage to root system. Healing starts immediately.

Courtesy of GCSAA.

A QUICK FIX

A ball landing on the green will likely leave an indentation. These indentations should be repaired. Like an airplane touching down on a runway, first contact may be far from where the ball eventually comes to a stop. After setting the bag down and pulling out the putter, locate and repair the pitch mark. Ball marks are litter. Help yourself to the good karma that comes from fixing someone else's mark.

○ Pick up your feet as you walk. Even with soft cleats, greens can be easily damaged.

FANCY FOOTWORK

A quick geometry review will come in handy navigating your way around the green: two points are connected by a straight line. Every ball will have its own path to the hole. Some putts will be shorter, others longer; some may take approximately the same route, but with four balls on the green, four imaginary and distinct lines exist. These lines extend from each ball to the hole. These are called putting lines. They're best noted and avoided. The reasoning is that a foot's imprint may adversely deflect a ball from its intended line; that is, it could deflect it from going in the cup. It is accepted courtesy in golf to avoid stepping on someone's line. Walk around the line or step over it. The issue is not quite what it was in the days of metal spikes or when greens weren't in such superb condition, but golfers still conscientiously observe the courtesy.

Sometimes stepping on a putting line can't be helped, especially as balls close in on the hole. There are two options: either mark the ball or putt out. Do so decisively. Others, sensing your indecision, may offer a "Don't worry about it. Go ahead and finish." Do so if you're ready. Otherwise mark the ball and carefully back out of the way. Let others finish before you re-mark and putt out.

Feet should remain outside a one-foot radius surrounding the hole, an especially important and sensitive area. Observing putting lines is one more demonstration of mindfulness and sportsmanship. Should you catch yourself stepping on someone's line—hey, it happens—a quick acknowledgment and apology should follow.

QUIET ON THE SET

Farthest out goes first—nothing new here. Before the sequence of putts begins, though, everyone is permitted a minute to stow their bag, trade out a wedge for a putter, fix a ball mark or two, find their ball, mark, and clean it. This grace period should not take as long as the line at the bank. Even if you've hit an outstanding shot and your ball lies inches from the hole, go tap it in or mark it. Expediently repair the pitch mark. Step aside to let others proceed. Be ready to putt out on cue.

Greens can be a pace-of-play train wreck. Hesitancy, indecision, an exaggerated sense of politeness and inexperience, whatever the reasons, some players freeze like deer in the headlights. We each have our own putt, but we prepare simultaneously, sharing the space. As always, it's imperative that golfers be ready to play without being prompted. The time to be absolutely still is when another golfer is poised to putt. Until then, take care of business quickly and efficiently.

Briskly completing the activities before putting (stowing the bag, repairing pitch marks, and so on) has its advantages. The sooner one gets to his ball, the more time one has to read (study) it. When new players stand around, unsure of what comes next, the pause is awkward. Experienced players don't relish playing crossing guard, nor do they enjoy having the natural flow of play disrupted. Here's how it so often occurs: One player putts past the hole. He then stands around, unsure of what to do. Ideally, after his first putt, he should go to his ball, mark it, step aside, and start considering the next putt. Should the ball stop close enough to the hole that the second putt is an easy one, he need only announce, "I'll finish," then do so. By the book, he is playing out of turn, but in recreational play this is for the greater good. In formal competition, doing so would invoke complications, but in this circumstance he should be encouraged. One player down, three to go. Who's up? Regardless of what happens, it's always someone's turn.

Distracted while putting—someone moving or talking or taking practice putts—wait until it stops. Anyone in your line of vision, or peripheral vision, should politely be asked to move. A glance may be all it takes. "Could you slide over so I can't see you?" should get the point across without causing offense.

The best putters are remarkably focused. Golf legend is filled with tales of champions oblivious to passing trains and blaring car horns. Often it's the little insidious sounds, coins jingling in a pocket or the slightest ill-timed movement, that really bug us.

Time between shots is well spent studying the green's contours. Looking over the undulation (in golfspeak: break) has been likened to reviewing a contract's fine print. Greens are rarely entirely flat. Knowing how hard to stroke a putt and determining how it will take a slope requires imagination, touch, and a steady hand. It can also waste time. Survey a putt while others are making theirs. All that should remain when it is your turn is to get into position, take a practice stroke, and pull the trigger. On those rare occasions when your ears ring with, "You're still away," steady the nerves, step up, and putt out.

TAKE A STAND

We stand by this: Golfers should not stand directly behind one another, especially on the green. This is common enough in team events, but normally it's considered a distraction and a breach of etiquette. Standing in front of someone putting, directly on the other side of the hole, is equally egregious. There will be times when it is advantageous to closely observe the roll of a putt on a similar line, a preview of your own. To do so, stand to the side out of the golfer's peripheral vision. Wait until the ball has been stroked, then and only then ease over to watch what happens. You're fine—as long as you wait until the ball leaves the putter before sliding behind to take a look.

STRIKE THE COLORS

Closest in tends the pin. The player whose ball is closest to the hole takes responsibility for pulling out the flagstick (mindful, naturally, to avoid stepping on prospective putting lines) and places it out of the way, preferably along the fringe. Never throw it. On long putts golfers have the option of having the staff attended (manned). To properly attend the flag, first take it out of the hole carefully so as not to damage the cup's earthen rim. Remember to avoid stepping in the area directly around the cup. Should the staff be stuck, tap it with a putter. It will give with a couple of firm taps. This also avoids the comedic embarrassment of tugging on the flagstick as the ball is rolling toward the hole, finding it stuck, and then yanking the cup from the ground. It's happened.

Hold the flagstick with one hand while standing on the same side as your shadow. The shadow should never obscure the hole. Grasp the flag to keep it from flapping. When the ball is struck, immediately remove the pin and step aside. Place it out of the way unless someone else needs it tended. There's no reason to wait until the ball closes in before pulling it. Televised golf shows caddies flawlessly executing pin duty.

To review:

1. Avoid stepping on putting lines.
2. Avoid stepping near the hole.
3. Avoid casting a shadow over the hole.

This may seem as painstaking as a Japanese tea ceremony, but there is more than protocol and custom at work. With respect to the area around the hole, there's a study that demonstrates the emergence of a wall around the cup. As the day wears on and golfers unconsciously press down the grass surrounding the cup, a "lumpy doughnut" develops that will prevent late afternoon putts from dropping. As much as we like doughnuts, we prefer them off the golf course.

A RULE TO REMEMBER

Attending the flag is a courtesy and an option for players putting from anywhere on the green. Those playing from just off the green must choose. The flagstick can be left in place or pulled. Hit the stick from on the green and it's a two-stroke penalty, a compelling reason for placing it out of the way. Hitting the flagstick from anywhere *off* the green, however, is fine. It's the individual's responsibility to decide how he wants it. Attending the flagstick should never be seen as an imposition. It's another of those things golfers do for one another.

ATTENTIVE ATTENDANCE

A common newbie mistake involves attending the pin. Some golfers will point out what they perceive as a putt's intended route to the hole by touching the ground. "Here's the line. Hit it here," they might say, touching the side of the cup. This is a definite no-no. As long as the putter hovers over the ground and does not touch the green, everything's copacetic. Occasionally a ball played from the fairway will collide with a ball on the green. No penalty is incurred. The first ball should be replaced in its original position. The other ball is played from where it stops. No harm, no foul.

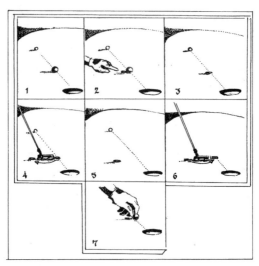

To move a mark, first place a coin behind your
ball (#2). Place your putter alongside (#4).
Transfer the coin (#5). Reverse the steps
(#6–7) before putting out.

MAKING YOUR MARK

Golfers mark their balls on the green as a courtesy, to clean
them, and to avoid causing a distraction or impediment. The
rules specify that a ball on the putting green must not hit anything but the hole. If my ball were to strike your ball, another
player's ball or the flagstick, I'd incur a two-stroke penalty.
It's my responsibility to ask anyone whose ball might even
remotely be in my line to mark.

When a golfer believes a ball is in her way, she requests
that it be marked. Any player may mark it when the ball is
on the green. Once marked, the ball can be cleaned before
being replaced to its original position. When it's obvious a
ball is in the way, mark it without delay. Another minute
saved.

One never minds being asked to mark and never hesitates asking. A coin, a golf glove snap, a plastic disc, any number of things will suffice. A tee is legal but discouraged. The preferred method of marking a ball is:

1. Place the mark behind the ball in relation to the hole.
2. Pick up the ball.

The most common mistake is to first pick up the ball, then put down the marker. To resume play, reverse the sequence: place the ball in front of the marker, pocket the mark.

ONE TO THE LEFT?

Depending upon the perceived route a ball may take to the hole, you may be asked to move your marker. It's not nearly as complicated as it sounds, just indicative of the lengths golfers go to respect their competitors. Mark your ball. Next, place the putter head alongside the mark.

Here's how it often happens. A player will say, "Please move it one to the left." That means one putter head to that side, again, to make sure the marker won't deflect the putt. If it happens, there's no penalty.

To accomplish this, pick up the mark and place it one putter head length away from the original position.

Now you're done, *except* that you must remember to backtrack your steps by returning the marker and the ball to its original position before putting. To avoid all this on very short putts, merely invite the golfer in the way to putt out.

○ **According to the rules, pitch marks anywhere on the green can be repaired. Cleat marks, however, cannot. Grass clippings, leaves, twigs, anything loose can be swept aside.**

It's unnecessary to ask a player if you should mark. He'll tell you. Either mark it or leave it. Calling attention to the ball is itself a distraction. It's the player's responsibility to request that the ball be marked. If there are any doubts, just mark it.

IS IT ME?

The golfer whose ball lies farthest from the hole plays first. It is, however, a common oversight to regard a ball anywhere on the green as closer when a ball just off the edge may actually be closer. In recreational golf play, golfers will routinely be invited to play onto the green before the formal putting sequence begins.

Who's away? A golfer with a 20-foot putt or a golfer 15 feet from the hole but off the green? The golfer with the 20-footer. It's his turn. He's farthest out. When someone invites you to play up, however, if you're ready, in the interests of time, go ahead, regardless of who's technically away.

DON'T STOP TILL YOU GET ENOUGH

Here's a welcome suggestion for speeding up the gridlock that can seize golfers on the green: putt out short putts rather than mark them. Just say, "I'll finish." Straddle a putting line if you must.

Continuous putting lets each golfer putt as long as it takes to finish. I go until I've holed out. Then you. Then Ed, then Elise. No turn taking. No marking. No time wasted determining who's away. The player farthest out starts, and the group proceeds, one by one, until everyone's done. Continuous putting, agreed upon in advance, or invoked when circumstances merit it, saves time. It may even help your putting.

THAT'S GOOD

"Gimmes," like mulligans, are outside the letter of the game's law, but they also save time. "That's good" usually accompanies a ball tapped back to the golfer. It's a tap-in, a putt assumed you'd make, and it counts a stroke. In recreational play putts are often conceded inside the leather—within a couple of feet of the hole. (Literally, in the space up to the grip when the putter is laid down on the ground from the hole. It's one of those golf sayings.)

Two provisos: Gimmes are never permitted in formal stroke-play tournaments. Then golfers must putt out. The same goes for anyone establishing a handicap. To avoid any unpleasantness, state your preference on the first tee or on the green. Tell the group you'd prefer to hole all your putts. Automatically kicking someone else's putt back is presumptuous. Better players, it must be said, can be impatient with new golfers in conceding putts. If it's a two-footer for a 6 or a 7, or higher, it's understandable, but no golfer should be denied the pleasure of hearing a par putt find the bottom of the cup.

Women frequently complain that men blithely tap putts back. Courtesy suggests that the person extending the freebie first ask, putter poised to return the ball. "May I give this to you?" or "That's good by me." If you'd rather not, *don't accept it*. No greater truism in golf exists than that the little ones count as much as the big ones. A two-inch putt counts the same as a 300-yard drive: one stroke. "Long ago," Bobby Jones recognized, "I learned that no putt is short enough to take for granted."

Golfers can easily lose track of each other's progress. Your putt's meaning may be lost to others, especially to those who, frankly, could care less. The sooner you are out of the way, to their thinking, the better. Yes, many golfers are prone to self-absorption. If the putt doesn't make any difference, gracefully accept a gimme. In match play, short putts are routinely conceded.

○ **When a putt finds the hole, retrieve it before the next player putts.**

FLY THE FLAG

The first golfer to finish retrieves and replaces the flagstick. With the last putt still rattling in the cup, the staff should be on its way back, the group collectively gathering up its stuff and moving toward the next tee. As the last player crouches over the putt, stand quietly. Resist the urge to creep in as he putts out. Stay out of his peripheral vision.

Golfers leaving the green together give a clear signal to those waiting in the fairway that it's safe to play. It's patently unfair to abandon the last player, leaving him with the added burden of sinking a testing putt, replacing the flag, and scurrying around to gather up his things and catch up.

HE SHOOTS! HE SCORES!

It's a textbook faux pas to tally up one's score on the green. Record it on the next tee as others prepare to tee off. There's always a moment to figure it out. Pull the cart away from the green so the following group can safely play in, taking yourself out of harm's way. Golfers are impatient with those who don't observe their position by decisively vacating the green. That includes the areas behind or to the side of the green.

A MOMENT OF SILENCE

Putting requires focus. One of P.G. Wodehouse's memorable characters blamed his missed putts on the "uproar of the butterflies in the adjoining fields." That's only a slight exaggeration.

"Among my many idiosyncrasies," wrote Richard Francis, "is the havoc whispers cause me when I have taken my stance, especially to putt. A passing train, the chimes of a nearby church are nothing; but the low murmur of a voice upsets my nerves and disposition, which is bad enough at best, and more often than not ruins the shot." Legions of golfers would agree.

NICE PUTT

A good putt, whether it's for three or for eight, is still a good putt. When someone compliments a shot, regardless of those disappointing blows that may have preceded it, a quick and cursory thanks is customary.

BRIEFING

- The green is a formal dining room where golfers are on their best behavior and play an active role in looking after the most expensive part of the course to maintain.

- Move decisively to your ball. Know when it's your turn. Fix pitch marks. Anticipate the flow of play.

- Use downtime to appraise putts.

- Be mindful of putting lines.

- Two areas to avoid: standing directly behind a golfer and standing directly in front of him on a line to the hole.

• Closest in tends the pin. First to hole out replaces it. Attending the pin, pull it out as soon as the putt is stroked, being careful not to damage the cup's brim. Place the flag out of the way.

• Mark a ball correctly: place the mark behind the ball, then pick up the ball. Not the other way around.

• Farthest away, first to play *unless* in the interest of time an opportunity presents itself.

• Continuous putting will shave minutes. Each golfer continues until the ball is in the cup. Easy.

• When a stroke is imminent, hold your ground. Stand quietly. No practice strokes.

• Quickly retrieve a ball from the hole after you've made your putt. Never dig the ball out of the hole with the putter.

• Tally up your score on the way to the next tee, any-where but on the green while others putt out.

> "Half of golf is fun, the other half is putting."
> —Peter Dobreiner, *The Hole Is More Than the Sum*
> *of the Putts*

HOLE	RATING/SLOPE	1	2	3	4	5	6	7	8	9	OUT
BLACK	72.0/128	402	154	390	561	396	169	433	408	378	3291
BRONZE	69.5/127	380	145	360	534	366	141	406	376	341	3049
GREEN	67.5/121	369	133	345	498	348	123	353	340	324	2833
PAR		4	3	4	5	4	3	4	4	4	35
HANDICAP		9	17	11	5	13	15	3	1	7	
RED	67.1/122	327	92	326	443	200	100	299	261	306	2354
Scorer:											

Quiz Time! Which hole is ranked No. 1 in difficulty? What's the par
for the fifth hole from the green tees? What's par for nine holes?
(Answers: The eighth, 4, 35.)

8 KEEPING SCORE

"How distinctive this feature of the game . . . It provides a universally level playing field for players of all levels of skill so that, for example, you or I can tee it up with Jack Nicklaus playing at the peak of his game. If you or I are playing at the peak of our own, our respective handicaps provide us with a reasonable chance of beating him.
—Frank "Sandy" Tatum Jr., *A Love Affair with the Game*

A new golfer needn't feel obligated to keep score. In the beginning, the more pressing concern is simply getting around the golf course in a timely manner. We learn to swim starting out on dry land mimicking the strokes. Only then do we get our feet wet, gradually becoming accustomed to a new environment. Golf is no different, except too many are left to sink or swim with disastrous results. Become used to being on a golf course. Learn the nuances of where to stand, taking turns, keeping up, and the fundamentals of play. Then, when you can (last pun) keep your head above water, move on to keeping score.

Score measures progress. Like an auction or the taking of one's temperature, it only records a brief window of time.

Take it for what it is: a snapshot, nothing more. The scorecard can be an imposing burden, especially for newcomers.

Professional golfers routinely play practice rounds where score is immaterial. Doing so familiarizes them with new courses: distances, greens, and the myriad options they'll face during the tournament. Forget the card for the same reason, to learn. Begin keeping score only after you've played a few times and know something of the distance you hit each club, and are comfortable with the social etiquette.

SCORING AT HOME

A scorecard is more than a place to write down who had what. It's a trove of information. It notes the par and length of each hole from each set of tees, the course rating, its difficulty (slope index), handicap rating, applicable local rules, and, occasionally, offers discount coupons for an oil change.

Actual yardage will differ somewhat from what's printed on the card. Tees are rotated to spare the grass and may slightly alter a hole's configuration. On par threes, especially, yardage markers in the ground will provide a more accurate indication of how long a hole plays.

SLOPE INDEX

Slope index is the result of a formula rating a course's relative difficulty, taking into account distance and the severity of obstacles from each set of tees. The information is useful in choosing the right tees. From the back tees, the slope index might be 140. *The higher the slope rating, the more difficult the course.* This will appear on the card in fine print, and it's the one new golfers should notice.

COURSE RATING

This is the rating expert golfers will look for. It suggests the score that a par-shooting (in golfspeak: *scratch*) golfer would have over the better half of his rounds. For instance, a course rating for a scratch golfer, from the back tees, may be 74.0, or, from the forward tees, 69.9. Again, it's enough to know that the higher the rating, the harder the course.

HANDICAPS

Handicaps are a way of projecting performance, an inexact science given the human factor. It's an imperfect system because, frankly, those who run it and those who use it are themselves imperfect. It assumes that everyone is trying their hardest to shoot their best every time out, and that's not always the case. Still, handicaps serve a useful purpose in providing a framework for competition, a pastime in golf as old as the game itself.

A handicap is an estimation of strokes taken over par. Assuming your average score on a course is 90, on a par 70 course, your handicap would be 20. This is simplistic calculation but handicaps are the average score shot over par. *The lower the score, the lower the handicap, the better the golfer.* It's worth noting that handicaps go up as well as down.

For a small fee any course will establish and maintain an approved handicap. They'll do the math and issue a card through the auspices of the USGA. A golfer turns in all his scorecards on any course, not just those rounds played on the course where the handicap is established. Only rounds played by the rules may be submitted. No mulligans and no gimmes. After twenty scores have been turned in (posted), the best ten are averaged and out pops a number and an index. The computations are complex, as are the number of variables: tees, course difficulty (slope), par for the expert (course rating). A handicap allows golfers to determine a benchmark for their skill that applies to any course. On one course a handicap might be 20, on a harder course, 25. It rises and falls, adjusted accordingly, and allows golfers the opportunity to play competitively in social and recreational settings.

Absolute beginning men start with a handicap of 36; women at 40. Scratch golfers or those with single-digit handicaps (1–10) are very good indeed. Qualifying in state and national championships typically requires handicaps of five or less.

The handicap line on the scorecard provides the key to allowing golfers to compete fairly for a match or wager. Here's how it works:

The first handicap hole (noted on the card with the numeral 1) is on the first, or front, nine holes. It can be any hole 1 to 9. The No. 2 handicap hole will be on the second, or back, nine holes—any hole 10 to 18. The No. 1 hole is considered the hardest hole on the front nine; the No. 2 handicap hole the most challenging hole on the back nine. So it goes down through the card—odd numbers on the front nine, even numbers on the back. Every course is ranked in this manner.

Why? So strokes can be "given" by competitors to even things out for the purposes of a match. Unless both golfers are the same handicap, the better golfer will give his opponent strokes. How many depends on their relative abilities.

Let's say we're playing a match. You're a 12 (handicap) and I'm a 15. To even the playing field, you give me a stroke on three holes, the numbers one, two and three handicap holes. That means I get a stroke on two holes on the front side, and one stroke for one hole on the back nine. Then we play.

In a stroke-team event, an 18-handicapper gets a stroke on every hole. A par on any hole will help the team in a scramble or best ball (see Chapter 10). A golfer with a 36-handicap gets two shots on every hole. So, a par on a par-3 hole—counting the handicap strokes—would go on the score-card as a one, an outstanding score.

Whether you decide to play seriously enough to pursue and maintain a handicap, it is imperative, not to mention socially correct, that golfers be honest about their score. Playing by the rules includes having an honestly acquired handicap. Some scoundrels inflate their handicaps in the hopes of getting more strokes than they'd otherwise be entitled in order to win prizes. Even the most technologically sophisticated system can't regulate character. There is a name for these people. They are known in golf as *sandbaggers.*

> "Physicists agree it is harder to hit a golf ball 100 yards over water than 200 yards over grass."　　　—Blackie Sherrod

9 GOLF RULES YOU SHOULD KNOW

Q. May a player open the doors of a barn to enable him to play a shot through the barn?

A. Yes. A barn is an immovable obstruction, but the doors are movable and may be opened.
— *Decisions of the Rules of Golf 2002–2003*

Once there were thirteen rules. Today there's a two-story building to assist golfers in interpreting them. Sacred text to some, arcane as the IRS code to others, the rules address a Pandora's Box of complexities; Rule 24-2b/15 above, for example.

The United States Golf Association (USGA) and the Royal and Ancient Golf Club of St. Andrews (R&A) write and administer the rules. The rules cover players, equipment, competition, the golf course, and the occasional barn door. The difficulty of interpreting and applying them has spawned a veritable cottage industry in translating the game's sense of fairness to the practical experiences of golfers.

The rulebook is not light reading, but some fun can be had in sitting down with the *Decisions Book*. This addendum to the rule book, revised every other year, fills in gaps for scenarios that are almost unimaginable. Balls rolling into drainpipes, lying next to half-eaten pears in bunkers (when there are no pear trees nearby, a key clue), snakes, fire ants, crawfish burrows, alligators, practical jokers—you name it, it's happened, and has subsequently been addressed. For mystery and suspense few bodice rippers rival this collection of the strange but true.

To be fair, adjudicating golf encompasses a changing universe. The game is played over hundreds of acres, in every natural environment, in all kinds of weather, across international borders, and over several hundred years. A set of rules issued during wartime in Great Britain bears out not only the unusual circumstances the rules must consider but the lengths to which golfers are prepared to go to play the game. They included the following provisions:

> In Competition, during gunfire and while bombs are falling, players may take cover without penalty for ceasing play.
>
> A player whose stroke is affected by the simultaneous explosion of a bomb may play another ball from the same place—penalty one stroke!

WHERE TO START

You will always be correct:

1. playing the ball as it lies.
2. playing the course as you find it.
3. not picking up your ball unless you know there's a rule that permits it.

These precepts have served golfers for centuries.

Many view the rules as unduly harsh They admittedly address unpleasant situations, and they can seem punitive.

The rules employ precise language to avoid creating confusion. The distinction that must be made concerns the type of golf being played on any given day. Is it competitive or recreational? It's like duplicate and social bridge. Competing in a tournament, where the rules exist in fairness to all players, is not the same as playing casually with friends. For those just getting started, certain liberties are permitted in the guise of maintaining a brisk pace of play. In competition there is no middle ground, no leeway no how with respect to the rules.

As athletes golfers take responsibility for their actions to an enviable degree. They officiate themselves, something unimaginable in pro sports. In the heat of high-stakes golf, competitors routinely call penalties on themselves. Playing by the rules remains a source of considerable pride in golf. If it sounds noble—calling penalties when no one else but the offending golfer has spotted the infraction—by today's standards, it most certainly is. Professional golfer Ben Crenshaw has commented that to him the rules are "sacred"; that's how serious they are to those who make their living playing the game.

"There are hazards and penalties in golf," he said. "And I'll tell you what. Golf will keep you on the straight and narrow." The rules and golf's unique regard for honesty underscore Ben's belief. Just imagine a close play at the plate in the seventh game of the World Series. In a cloud of dust the umpire calls the runner safe. Now imagine the likelihood of the runner jumping up, dusting himself off and saying, "No, I was out. He tagged me first." That's how different golf is.

THE SAME PAGE

The rules provide a basis for those who choose to assay a modest wager, putting competitors "on the same page." This is also a venerable tradition. Whether you care to bet or not, we certainly encourage learning the rules. The game is more satisfying when they are observed. For many golfers there is no other way of playing.

As with etiquette, the rules offer clarity. Comfort comes in doing the right thing. This alone is fortifying. Golf would not be nearly as enticing without adversity, which remains a cherished aspect of golf, a game in which there is no one else to blame. The ball only goes where we hit it. Those who play golf respect and abide by the rules and in turn are accorded respect for observing them, even when the call doesn't go their way. Open the Rules of Golf and you will see the importance etiquette merits. The first section is entitled "Courtesy on the Course."

The following are suggestions of rules you should know (written in language, we hope, that is less foreboding than the official text). An updated copy of the rules can be procured at any golf course, and, at least for the time being, is still small enough to conveniently fit in a golf bag or on a nightstand. These suggestions are not a replacement for the rulebook, merely an introduction to those rules most frequently encountered. For serious diversion we recommend the *Decisions Book*. Other pertinent rules are covered in context.

TEEING GROUND

On the teeing ground (informally known as the tee box), the ball must be teed behind the markers within two club lengths. Any club may be used to measure. One's feet do not have to be positioned inside the markers; the ball, however, does.

Should the ball accidentally be knocked off the tee while addressing it or in taking a practice swing, replace it without penalty. Even if the ball goes forty yards down the fairway, if it was an accident, start over with a clean slate. With the intention of hitting it, however, should the ball squirt out to the right forty yards, that's where it must be played.

OUT OF BOUNDS

The boundaries of the golf course, or any part of the course, are marked by white stakes or lines. Beyond the lines is out of bounds. When a ball goes out of bounds, the golfer is required to replay the shot. (This is referred to as stroke and distance.)

Return to where the original shot was played. Counting: It's one, the original shot—two, for the penalty—now playing three. Out of bounds protects overzealous golfers from potentially dangerous and delicate situations. Houses along golf courses are marked by stakes as "OB." So are the driving range, streets, cliffs, pastures, pool decks, etc.—but not always barns! Even if the ball is an inch outside the imaginary line that connects the stakes, it's out of bounds.

After teeing off, should the ball appear to have gone out of bounds, momentarily step aside. Let the others play their drives, then retee. You're now hitting your third shot.

> "There is no surer or more painful way to learn a rule than to be penalized once for breaking it."
> —Tom Watson, *The Hole Is More Than the Sum of the Putts*

LOST BALL

The rules specify that when a ball is lost, the golfer must return to the spot where the original ball was played and play on. It counts just like a ball hit out of bounds. One for the original shot, two for the penalty, now playing three.

This is routinely sloughed off by recreational players to save time. Golfers will often drop a ball at the spot where they think the ball vanished and play from there. Misunderstandings about golf rules often occur when an experienced player, in the interest of saving time, breaks a rule. To the inexperienced it appears that's how golf is played. To avoid any confusion, players breaking a rule (remember, only in recreational golf) might announce something like, "This is not by the rules, but I'm going to do it since we've fallen behind."

Competing in tournaments or in establishing or maintaining a handicap, the rule—every rule—must be observed. You must take your medicine. If the ball can't be found—there's a five-minute grace period—go back and put another ball into play.

PROVISIONAL

When one suspects a ball may be lost or out of bounds, after others have teed off, a *provisional* may be played. This is not a mulligan—a freebie and a liberal exception to the rules. Provisionals must be announced. "I think I'd better hit another one" is insufficient. You must say, "I'll hit a provisional." Should you find your first ball, in bounds, play it. Pocket the provisional. If the original ball is gone, play the provisional, which becomes your third shot. A provisional can be played anywhere on the golf course.

UNPLAYABLE LIE

An *unplayable* can be taken anywhere outside a water hazard. It's each player's call. Rather than risk damaging a club or a wrist or wasting several shots, for the cost of one stroke, a golfer may move the ball two club-lengths in any direction as long as it is not moved closer to the hole. This may not seem like much of a bargain, but it may be prudent, particularly after the ball remains unmoved after several swings. There are two other options:

1. Return to the original scene of the unfortunate stroke and put another ball into play.

Or

2. Retreat on a line as far back as you like, keeping the spot where the ball lies between you and the flagstick.

The penalty is one stroke. One in, two for the penalty, playing three out.

RELIEF

Relief, often referred to as a *free drop*, is permitted when one's ball comes to rest on a cart path, in what's known as *casual water* (standing water from rain or sprinklers), on an anthill, a sprinkler head, or is interfered with by any man-made object: water fountains, benches, etc. (An exception: Out-of-bounds markers, firmly in the ground, are considered permanent fixtures. No relief is given.)

To take relief, first determine the *nearest point of relief*. It is the spot as near as possible to the ball's original position, no closer to the hole, that does not interfere with the swing or stance. Drop within one club length of that point. This rule is also invoked when a proper stance cannot be assumed because of a sprinkler head, cart path, etc. Relief cannot be taken because a tree is in the way; only if a man-made object interferes with the swing or stance. The same relief is offered for *ground under repair* (marked by a white line).

CHEATING

Cheating is childishly easy in golf. Deliberately recording a five instead of a six on the scorecard, improving a ball's lie in the rough, replacing a marked ball closer to the hole—there are a million and one ways that no one is likely to catch. There are a lot of golfers, including some good ones, who cheat. Playing in a stroke play event, competitors have to accept it as an obligation to stop and prevent golfers from taking advantage.

Several distinctions need first be made before someone's branded. *Cheating is the deliberate intent to deceive.* It is not an oversight, an accident, or a misunderstanding.

A distinction must also be made with respect to casual and tournament play. They're not the same. In a recreational round gimmes may be offered, lies improved, liberties taken. Only the individual is affected, not the other players, the *field*, were it an actual tournament. With wagers involved, no matter how small, everyone should at least play by the same rules, even if they aren't strictly USGA.

In formal events there are no degrees of honesty or ignorance. An infraction either occurred or it didn't. In casual rounds the only golfer really being cheated is the culprit. Should someone choose to mark down five when you know he had eight, don't bet them for lunch or a drink after the round. If it annoys you, find other people to play with. One of the most popular players at one club asks in recreational play, after each hole, not "What did you have?" but "What do you want?"

In tournaments, every player is obligated to ensure that the event is fairly played, whether it's the Eastside Possum Club Halloween Invitational or the PGA Championship. Those uncomfortable with confronting others over an alleged infraction should report it to the pro cither at the turn or at the end of the round. There are several advantages to bringing it up right then and there. First, the player may not be aware of the mistake. Also, it prevents the transgression from being repeated. It gives the player the opportunity to rectify the error in context: he might play another ball, for instance, rather than risk disqualification when it's too late to do anything about it. (Once a golfer has signed the scorecard, attesting that it's correct, it's too late for corrections should there have been a mistake. Several famous tournaments have unfortunately been lost because of incorrect scorecards.)

Disputes can be settled immediately with a ruling or by playing out two balls to the satisfaction of the disputing parties. The committee, or the pro, can sort it out later. Golf isn't a matter of life and death, but, by the same token, honesty is not just something that we practice for the sake of convenience. *A golfer is only as good as his word.*

New golfers need not fear accusations of cheating. Moving the ball to a better location, or other training-wheel-type advantages are permissible—as long as every attempt is made to play in a timely manner.

As proficiency moves beyond the beginning stages, we recommend the goal of strict adherence to the rules. There is an undeniable sense of satisfaction that comes from knowing you're playing the right way. Every golfer savors the accomplishment of having successfully pulled off a tough shot, playing the ball as it lies, as golf has been played for centuries. It's a great feeling. "You play the game by the rules and that in itself is an infallible mark of a gentleman of quality," Tommy Armour observed. "Nobody ever cheats anybody else at golf. The one who is cheated is the one who cheats."

BRIEFING

• A copy of the official rules or the *Decisions on the Rules of Golf* can be purchased from golf courses or the United States Golf Association:

> USGA
> Liberty Corner Road
> P.O. Box 708
> Far Hills, NJ 07931
> (908) 234-2300
> http://www.usga.org

The USGA also publishes a handy pocket-size summary of some principal rules, "Golf Rules in Brief." It's easier to understand than the Rule Book. There are also numerous books to help golfers learn and better appreciate the rules.

• For a lost ball or one hit out of bounds (count along!), it's:

> A-one for the original shot,
> A-two for the penalty, and,
> A-three for the shot you're now playing.

That's "stroke and distance."

> Q. A ball lodges against a dead land crab in a bunker. May the crab be removed without penalty?
> A. A dead land crab is a natural object and thus a loose imped-iment and not an obstruction. Removal of the crab would be a breach of Rule 13–4.
>   Rule 23/6 Dead Land Crab (*Decision on the Rules of Golf*)

10 PLAYING IN A TOURNAMENT

"When you have any bit of hard luck, don't keep talking about it for several holes afterward. . . . The more you talk about such things the more he [your opponent] thinks that you are getting old and cranky and really rather a nuisance to play with."

—H. J. Whigham, *The Common Sense of Golf* (1910)

They can be combined with other formats but there are basically two kinds of tournaments: stroke and match. (Stroke is also referred to as medal play.) In stroke play, golfers compete against a field for the lowest overall score. In match play, as in tennis, golfers compete head-to-head in a series of elimination rounds. Most pro events are four rounds of stroke play. The winner has the lowest score after 72 holes.

A natural vehicle for charities, golf tournaments go with business like scotch and soda. They combine a friendly, competitive environment with networking opportunities and a worthy cause. There's room for the skilled as well as the casual golfer to take part. Here's where handicaps come into play, as they're used to form equitable teams. High handicappers will always be welcome partners in team formats thanks to the quality of their companionship, certainly, but also for the number of strokes they'll receive. Not having a handicap will exclude participation in many events, but not all, as the new golfer can be assigned a handicap. The bottom line remains a chance to get away from the office in a pleasant setting and to help those in need.

The most popular formats go by various names but are essentially either a scramble or shamble.

Scramble. The team, typically composed of four golfers, has four chances to hit a great shot. Everyone tees off. The best shot is selected. Players retrieve their balls and play on from the most advantageous position. All play their second shot and again the best position is selected. Play continues in this manner until the ball drops into the cup. Occasionally, a rule will be added to make things more interesting by requiring each team member to contribute two drives during the round. This prevents the team from relying too heavily on one player, adding an element of teamwork and strategy.

Shamble. A variation on the scramble, all players tee off. The best drive is selected, as above, but here's the difference: each golfer then completes the hole playing his own ball from the site of the preferred drive. Golfers who are not going for a score of par or better pick up.

TOURNAMENT GLOSSARY

There are an endless number of ways to compete at golf. The following primer provides the basics. Interesting and wondrously complex, betting is covered in the chapter on business golf. In every organized event, there will be a rules sheet likely posted in each cart and covered by the tournament director before the round. Read the sheet. Invariably it includes points of interest, from local rules to cart policies on certain holes.

Medal (or Stroke) Play. Every stroke counts. Each golfer plays his or her own ball. The lowest total score wins.

Match Play. The oldest form of competition. Each hole represents an individual match. The winner of the first hole goes "one up," and no matter whether he wins the hole by one shot or five, he only wins that one hole. The match continues. Holes that are ties are said to be "halved." The match ends when one player is more holes "up" than there are holes left to play. The golfer who wins his match 4&3, for example, was four holes up with three holes to play.

Best Ball. Team format for either two or four players in which golfers play out the hole with their own ball and the best score, or two scores, are recorded.

Stableford. A popular format overseas whereby points are awarded in accordance with notable play. A birdie might be worth five points, a par worth three points, a bogey one point. An extraordinary shot, say, an eagle (two under par—a three on a par 5) might be worth seven points, a hole-in-one nine. This is the one format where the highest score wins.

Four Ball. In the U.S., it refers to four players each playing her own ball and recording her own score. In Great Britain, it means a match of two against two. When one player has made or appears certain to record a score on a hole that the other team cannot top, the partner out of the hole *picks up* (stops).

Foursome. Teams of two golfers compete against each other with partners alternating shots until the ball is holed. Sometimes called a Scotch foursome, it's a venerable part of international competitions like the Ryder, Walker, Solheim, and Curtis Cups. Not for the meek.

Gross. The actual score recorded before being adjusted by handicap. Were you to shoot a 101, that would be your gross score.

Net. The score after being adjusted. A gross 95 with a 14 handicap becomes a net score of 81.

Old Tom Morris, the ancient and revered keeper of the green of the famed Old Course at St. Andrews, Scotland, is laid to rest in a nearby churchyard. It's worth recalling his epitaph in thinking about competitive golf. It reads: "Modest in victory, generous in defeat." That neatly sums up the great golfers, champions in every sense of the word.

YOUR MOMENT IN THE SUN

Before pro tournaments, as an exciting fund-raising perk for sponsors, a tournament within a tournament is held. It pairs a team of amateurs with a touring pro. Typically a one-day event, the *pro-am* provides an opportunity to spend some quality time on the golf course with one of the game's best. The pro-am has produced the most recent change in etiquette— what's being called "par as your partner." Slow play is crippling professional golf, and it has long been a problem in pro-ams. Amateurs are being asked to pick up as soon as they've reached a "net par" score, at the point where they can no longer help their team. "When a player pumps a tee shot out of bounds," an official suggests, "he probably shouldn't reload when his professional partner and teammates are in the fairway. Little things like that can speed up a round."

WATCHING THE PROS

Golf is special in many respects. Pro golf is especially notable for allowing spectators to get remarkably close to the action. Only a rope separates competitors from fans. Patrons, as they're known at the venerable Masters tournament, need to be aware of the consequences of their actions and movements when

BYRON NELSON
Classic

May 1, 2002

Dear Gold Pro-AM Participant,

Please allow me this opportunity to discuss a new directive from the PGA TOUR with regards to pace of play for Pro-Ams. We are trying to take a proactive approach to a serious problem that if not corrected, could affect your enjoyment at our Pro-Ams and could further affect our charity.

As you may know, pace of play has become an important issue on TOUR and it affects TOUR players as well as the Pro-Ams that take place before the tournament competition begins. (See enclosed article) The PGA TOUR has instructed TOUR events that Pro-Am rounds must finish no more than one-half hour longer than normal TOUR rounds. This means a goal of 4 ½ hours. The penalty would be severe, resulting in a reduction of available Pro-Am playing spots in future tournaments.

Proper pace of play is necessary for any enjoyable round of golf. Etiquette would dictate that we follow a few simple rules:

1. Be Ready To Hit – We do not want you to deviate from normal shot routine, but do have your club selected and strategy planned.

2. Stay With The Pack - Keep up with group in front of you.

3. Fight Another Hole – Par is your Partner in the Pro-Am; pick up your ball if you are out of the hole. Remember, this is a team competition.

4. Do Not Spend Time Looking – If your ball seems lost, let it go and play another. You will not run out of balls, we will make sure of that.

The Verizon Byron Nelson Classic is proud to be a leader on TOUR in money provided to charity with more than $64 million raised since 1973. The Pro-Am events are a large reason why the Salesmanship Club Youth & Family Centers can provide the services it does each year. If we fail to meet the TOUR's standards on Pro-Ams, it clearly means less money available for the services that are provided to over 3,500 children and families in the Dallas area.

Assisting in the process will be a number of our members on the course serving as walking marshals and ball spotters throughout your round. They will be present to assist you in achieving the 4 ½ – hour goal. We appreciate your commitment to our tournament and we know that by ensuring a proper pace of play it will enhance your participation in the Pro-Am.

Finally, I would like to remind everyone that the Gold Draw on Monday, May 6th has been moved from the Hotel Inter-Continental to the Convention Center at the Adam's Mark Hotel (400 N. Olive St.) in Dallas. Cocktails will begin at 6 p.m. and the draw will follow promptly at 7 p.m.

Thanks in advance for your help in assuring a great Pro-Am.

Sincerely,

Frank Swingle

Frank Swingle
Tournament Chairman

May 5-12, 2002 ♥ Benefiting the Salesmanship Club Youth and Family Centers

verizon

Salesmanship Club of Dallas ♥ 400 South Houston Street ♥ Suite 350 ♥ Dallas, Texas 75202-4811 ♥ (214) 742-3896 ♥ FAX (214) 742-3899

www.scdallas.org ♥ www.byronnelson.pgatour.com

golfers are at work, as the golf course truly is the golfers' office.

One year at the Masters, the crowd showed an unsporting partisanship that troubled tournament scion Bobby Jones. He penned the following timeless guidelines that have, ever since, been reprinted on the daily tournament pairing sheets and tickets.

> In golf, customs of etiquette and decorum are just as important as rules governing play. It is appropriate for spectators to applaud successful strokes in proportion to difficulty but excessive demonstrations by a player or his partisans are not proper because of the possible effect upon other competitors.
>
> Most distressing to those who love the game of golf is the applauding or cheering of misplays or misfortunes of a player. Such occurrences have been rare at the Masters but we must eliminate them entirely if our patrons are to continue to merit their reputation as the most knowledgeable and considerate in the world.

SUGGESTIONS

> No matter how well you may know a player, do not accost him on the golf course. Give him a chance to concentrate on his game. Walk—never run. Be silent and motionless when a contestant prepares to execute a stroke. Be considerate of other spectators. Golf is a gentlemen's game.

Crowd behavior continues to be a concern. "There's nothing wrong with the fans showing enthusiasm," Tiger Woods said following the 2002 U.S. Open, "just as long as they're respectful. Being respectful is what separates our sport from the others."

JUNIOR GOLF

David Kite, son of Champions and PGA Tour great Tom Kite, plays on his high school golf team. He kindly shared his impressions from participating at top-level junior golf. Most of his comments were positive, but he expressed concerns of interest to prospective players, parents, and coaches.

Golf shares the unfortunate problems familiar to organized sports, including overzealous parents. There are those parents who pressure their kids to perform to their own (often high) expectations, and those who stretch the limits in seeking every advantage. They want to give advice, suggest certain clubs to hit, correct a swing fault, or otherwise inject themselves into disputes or misunderstandings with the rules.

Often parents don't know the rules of golf, and fewer should get involved with decisions. Parents devote time and money to junior programs to allow youngsters an opportunity to experience the game. Most parents, coaches, and sponsors are dedicated, generous, and selfless individuals who enjoy promoting participation in a sport that can be enjoyed over a lifetime. It's a few who cause problems.

Most kids, if asked, David said, would advise parents to "stay out of the way." Teach kids etiquette as they learn the game along with a few rules so parents won't be tempted to intervene. When a twelve-year-old miraculously qualified for the U.S. Open, no one questioned her skill or determination. The only criticism she received concerned her blind spots regarding proper etiquette. Her game was mature. Sadly, her manners weren't.

THE VOICE OF EXPERIENCE

The following appeared on a country club bulletin board, it happened to be in Texas, but the sentiments are universal, no

Shamble, scramble, pro-am, there's room for the skilled as well as the casual golfer to participate in tournaments.

doubt born of bitter experience. Our thanks to the anonymous author who we hope feels much better now.

You are my partner for today, not by choice. I probably got you in a blind draw or perhaps nothing better was available. I think I know what the objective of the game is. So please . . .

Don't tell me to take my time on any putts.
Don't tell me to knock it in.
Don't tell me to get it up there.
Don't tell me we need this.

IF I WANT ANY ADVICE I WILL ASK FOR IT. SO UP UNTIL THAT TIME, KEEP YOUR DAMNED MOUTH SHUT.

"Provided there is a clear hole ahead of you, you must not clog the course if the match following you is waiting to go through, but beckon them to play through. Do the same in the event of a lost ball." —*Golf Penalties and Etiquette* (1904)

Even a five-time Tour de France winner needs to
know his etiquette.

11   BUSINESS GOLF

"Some people are more 'touchy' than others, particularly in so infuriating a pastime as golf, and I hope I may say, without appearing to be preaching a sermon, that it is up to each of us to make allowances for the other man's foibles."

—Henry Longhurst, *How to Get Started in Golf* (1967)

A partner in one of the nation's largest venture capital firms, Joe Aragona, also happens to be a golfer. Joe calls golf "the doctrine of continuous dealing."

"You're always trying to make a deal work," he believes. "It's part of business to assume you're going to play again and again to establish a relationship." Etiquette is hardly an affectation. "You just can't afford the embarrassment or discomfort in any business," he says, "whether it's in the office or on the golf course."

Former software CEO Russ Caccamisi, one of Joe's regular playing partners, adds that customer golf requires a "greater sensitivity than the weekend round with your friends. Most importantly, remember why you are there," he says; "if you are there to sell, make sure the environment is conducive to selling."

A check of any executive's speed dial confirms the merger

between golf and corporate America. Who's on it? Family, stockbroker, doctor, lawyer—and golf buddies. Golf provides a means of access, rapport—and, yes, unimpeachable insight. Four hours spent knocking it around reveals an individual's and even a company's character, culture, attitude, and ethics like few other casual endeavors.

Shell Oil President, Chairman, and CEO Steven L. Miller talked with the authors about golf's corporate role during the PGA Tour's Shell Houston Open.

Q: Have you ever actually closed a deal on the golf course?
Miller: Absolutely, the golf course, sitting around just before or after, has probably been the most frequent place where I have done deals.

I find that when you do difficult negotiations it's always better to do them in an informal setting rather than a formal setting, and a golf course is an ideal setting. And, besides, once you spend some time with people, you get to know them and that's what golf lets you do. It makes those hard decisions easier to make when you've had a chance to know somebody, be with them, have some fun with them, and that's why the setting works like it does.

We've placed client golf near the end because etiquette learned and practiced in recreational and social golf will successfully guide you in playing with clients, team members, the boss, or prospective employers the world over. That's one of the payoffs that comes from observing the game's customs; they transcend cultural, generational, and geographical boundaries. The bottom line is forming meaningful working relationships, finding common ground. Golf offers a conducive climate without the pain and expense of, say, corporate retreats, a week in the woods, or—help us—rope obstacle courses.

Doing business with someone trustworthy can't help but

inspire a greater belief in his or her product or investment. Those in sales quickly recognize golf as a useful avenue to finding and engaging clients. Professional women, once they look past golf as merely recreational (and see how welcome they are as scramble partners) find it a fertile source of leads. And it's so much more desirable than a late night dinner after a full day in the office.

SETTING THE AGENDA

A guest deserves to know the drill. Tee time, walking or riding, lunch—would that be before or after golf? Is there a different dress code in the men's grill than on the golf course? Anything you'd want to know were the roles reversed should be laid out well in advance, from dress code to format, partners to handicaps, down to shirt sizes (for presents). Some clubs have relaxed their requirements on golf shoes and jeans. Some never will. Others insist on a coat and tie and, please, no hats or caps in the dining room. If this information is not forthcoming, guests, to avoid surprises, should pick up the phone and call the golf shop. (Those walking, with a caddie, might also want to shift to a lighter, more manageable bag.) The social miscues resulting from letting the chips fall can be infamous and painful. And no two clubs operate the same.

I GOT IT

The person extending the invitation, in other words the host, picks up the tab.

THE HOST

- *Always* takes care of green fees, caddies fees, cart fees, on-course refreshments. Caddie tips may be split, but nothing else. It's the host's show.
- Makes sure everything is taken care of in advance. No surprises.
- Determines the intensity and skill levels of the group and adjusts attitude accordingly. Doesn't impose a by-the-book severity on golfers who play once a year. In the spirit of camaraderie, commerce, and pace of play, he overlooks the occasional *foot wedge* (picking up or moving to a better spot)—with the stipulation that the round cannot be counted in establishing a handicap.
- Sets the tone for the outing, from the seriousness to the schedule, to mulligans and gimmes.
- Picks the appropriate tees with an eye to not put undue pressure on weaker players.
- Proposes teams and bets, if any. (Read on.)
- Decides when it's appropriate to talk shop.

THE GUEST

- Always offers to pay his way. If, or more likely when, the host offers to pick up the tab, be gracious but never take it for granted.
- When the beverage cart arrives, offers to pick up refreshments.
- Is punctual and appropriately dressed, the consummate professional.
- Follows the host's lead from the practice range to the 19th hole with respect to the seriousness of the round.
- Never patronizes the host by deliberately playing poorly or losing.

- Leaves the cell phone in the car or on silent mode. The pro shop can be alerted to potential emergencies and can be trusted to relay important messages.
- Graciously accepts a gimme or a mulligan.
- Observes proper etiquette and, above all, plays in a timely manner, maintaining an awareness of and interest in the welfare and play of others.
- Never loses sight of the ultimate objective: This is a business meeting and a business result is expected.

One last word about who pays: When both parties offer to pay, there may be a momentary awkwardness, but at least the matter's settled. One of you will take care of it. The alternative is a potentially embarrassing situation in which no one does, brought to light by the arrival of an assistant pro in the parking lot asking for the unpaid green fees.

Since there is no such thing as fashionably late in golf, guests will naturally be on time, just as they would for an appointment or interview. Arrive early. As Shell's Steven Miller suggests, the time before and after the round offers opportunities for meaningful exchanges. Know too that many golfers have strong feelings about mixing golf and business. Some prefer not to sully their golf with mundane matters.

WARMING UP

Hitting some balls first is always a good idea. For this round, it also allows everyone a glimpse of what's in store. We hesitate to say it—but if there is no range available, or practice is just not in the cards—a mulligan on the first tee may be necessary to get things off to a good start, but *never* suggest or take a *mully* when the course is crowded.

If the host is serious about his golf, then—at least for today—you are, too. If the day is merely to be a good walk spoiled, then don't treat it as the final round of the U.S. Open. Follow the host's cue. Remember, for today, golf is the conduit to establishing common ground.

A little flexibility (no pun intended) while warming up may also be prudent. For the sake of convenience, modify your practice routine and fall in behind the host. You may prefer to putt first before hitting balls. Today, head to the range. Time spent stretching or stroking a few putts together is time well spent.

THE FIRST TEE

A few points of order before the round gets underway. The arrangements will already be set with respect to who rides together and who drives. These can be amended, say, after nine holes, if need be, to give everyone a chance to visit. The first tee is also the place to discuss local or *winter rules*—whether everyone is going to be allowed to improve a lie in the fairway or play it *down* (as it lies)—basically, setting ground rules.

Expert players, as hosts, should move up to the forward tees in deference to less accomplished golfing guests. Why force weaker players out of their comfort level? This isn't about showing up a client by playing the *tips* (back tees). It isn't about winning a golf match against someone who couldn't hit the fairway with a cannon. Remember the big picture. What happens on the course is a prelude, an introduction. The host's role is to take care of his guests, and that may mean playing the front tees. Teams could conceivably be split to accommodate skill levels. One player from each cart can play the white tees, say, and one player plays the black tees. The point is to keep things light and easy.

Some people obviously thrive on the competition. Others would rather just play. Feel your way. If Warren Buffett and Bill Gates, two of the richest men in the world, only play for a dol lar, high stakes are not exactly critical to having a spirited match. Golfers often do play "for a little something," one of golf's oldest traditions as some of the game's earliest writing attests.

○ Try to avoid filling out a foursome with another noninvolved player. (Another reason to check in well in advance of the golf date.) Unless it's peak time (weekend mornings), a twosome or threesome will likely be allowed. A "third wheel" can be awkward for everyone.

BETTING

The most common wagers are nassaus. They entail three bets: one for the first nine holes, a bet for the score on the back nine, and a bet for the total score. If the bet is a $5 nassau, it's $5 for the winning score on the front, $5 for winning the back, and $5 for winning the total. The most the bettor can lose is $15. Then there is the *press*. If one team pulls out ahead, it's a new bet, double-or-nothing. Say your team is two holes down. You press and win the next hole. You're now even. The match is squared. With money at stake, not to mention honor, everyone needs to be on the same page with respect to the rules, whatever has been agreed upon. Sure, it's only a few bucks, but it's in these exchanges that character is revealed. Whether it's twenty five cents or a thousand dollars, the golfer who does not pay off a bet—put it this way—is that the kind of person you want to do business with? Whatever transpires, *never ever fail to pay off a bet*.

It can get complicated. There's an astonishing number of ways to wager. Some common side bets, known as *trash* or *junk*:

Greenies—paid off on par threes to the one closest to the hole on the tee shot.

Sandies—a bonus to "getting up and down" from a bunker with one shot and one putt.

Barkies—hit a tree and still make a par.

If the nassau is for $5, the above side bets are typically for a little less, say $1. There are many games. *Skins* are won when a golfer has the best score on a hole. If two players tie, all tie, and the pot carries over until someone finally wins a hole outright. On one hole, you may be pulling for one player to sink a putt to cover a score. On the next hole, it may be you against the others. There's *Wolf*, where players choose up sides on each hole on the basis of their tee shots, and *Bingle, Bangle, Bongle,* where points are awarded: one for the first player to reach a green (bingle), one for the shot closest to the hole (bangle), one for the first player in the hole (bongle). With so many games going, to be one of the guys, learn the most popular.

Playing for a little something means different things. Big-money games have long been a source of golf legend. Lee Trevino, the popular professional, who came from an impoverished background, noted that pressure is playing for $10 when you have a dime in your pocket. His contemporary, the flashy Doug Sanders, once laid down the following ground rules:

Never gamble to hurt a friend.
Never gamble outside your comfort zone.
Never needle, harass, or poke fun at a playing partner on the edge of despair.
Never fail to settle your debts immediately after a round.
If you win, be gracious.

To which Russ Caccamisi adds this cautionary advice: Leave it alone. Betting can provide a distraction, even an edge to the round that could cause lingering hard feelings, not exactly the desired result of a successful business golf outing. His bottom line:

> If you have a choice, DO NOT WAGER . . . betting adds a level of intensity and competitiveness to the typical business round that detracts from the purpose of the round—business. This is not to say you can't have a friendly game of Wolf or Skins with business associates . . . just make sure that you do not diminish the business relationship by taking some of your fellow player's money on the golf course, create animosity (whether you think you do or not), and jeopardize taking the money you really want—their business.

Why risk a $2 million deal to win $2? Ouch.

WHEN TO TALK SHOP

When the client broaches the subject. With this thought: conversation should not interfere with the group's obligation to keep pace, nor with one's effort to concentrate and hit good shots. When the cart stops and the player selects a club and begins going through the motions, that's not the time to float the merger trial balloon. Same for the moment the group in front clears the green, or just before a twenty-footer. There will always be time—in the cart leaving the green, at the turn, searching for a ball, etc.—to bond. The 19th hole, after the round, was made for downtime.

○ Ever notice that those who try to impress others with their prominence never succeed? Nor are they a joy to be around, especially on the golf course. The truly important never feel that compulsion.

KEEPING PLAY MOVING

The golfer who knows the course will have useful insight. Pointing out the routing for a hole, for instance, can be helpful in a general sense, but no one needs to hear seemingly well-intended advice.

Conceding short putts will also save time, and be a relief to the less experienced; the hardcore golfer, however, may resent the implication—he typically putts everything out. When *everything* is for another seven, or an eight, or higher, and golfers are wearily taking practice swings back in the fairway, nothing is served by prolonging the agony. Gimmes can be gratefully accepted. Count it as one stroke. Four with a gimme putt makes five. Try and keep abreast of how the others are doing, to be quick with a "Nice par" or "Good five" when appropriate. It demonstrates an admirable consideration for others beyond the amnesiac cloud that envelopes all of us on the golf course. Should you replace someone's divot with a scoop of mix or instinctively move to search for another's wayward ball, you're demonstrating an ability to look beyond the fray and act in a considerate manner that will be duly noted and appreciated.

DISCRETION

Golf is an extended interview. How adversity is handled speaks volumes about one's ability to weather a storm. The care shown the course, equipment, the tender area around the cup in replacing the pin, and, yes, one's reaction to bad shots, may determine the course of the relationship. The golfer who plays slowly may be the same person perennially late in meeting deadlines. There are those who believe that the swing itself reveals something of one's personality. First impressions are always important, and golf provides innumerable challenges and insights (and comic relief). Also, with respect to profanity, put it this way: If it would be inappropriate in a general client meeting, it's probably inappropriate on the golf course. Among old friends is another matter.

> "If profanity had an influence on the flight of the ball, the game would be played far better than it is."
> —Horace Hutchinson, *Golf: A Turn-of-the-Century Treasury*

TAKING FLIGHT

Colorful U.S. Open champion Tommy Bolt suggested that when overtaken by an urge to throw a club, the offending implement should always be hurled forward to save going back for it. A timesaving tip, perhaps, but the tantrum is best suppressed, if only for the cumulative pall it casts over others.

Barbara once had a student who let loose after just a few swings—during a lesson. "Um, perhaps we better start with the mental approach," she suggested.

"The satisfaction gained from a horrifying display of temper on the golf course—one where you might have broken every club in your bag, sworn in five languages, and taken a foot-long divot out of the green," observes writer Lauren St. John, "is short and bittersweet, and all you are left with is a sick and guilty feeling in the pit of your stomach because you know you've violated a kind of sacred code."

THE 19TH HOLE

After the round is the time to exchange business cards, relax over a drink, and relive past battles. If your host does not order anything alcoholic, follow suit. It's likely that with everyone together and comfortable business discussions will take place in earnest.

BUSINESS TOURNAMENTS

Many clubs sponsor member-guest events. These are always handicap tournaments with flights based on the relative abilities of the competitors. They're often dispensed as premiums, to repay good accounts or to develop closer ties. There are golfers whose handicaps seem to fluctuate according to the situation. The member must be certain a guest's handicap is accurate, or risk suffering guilt by association from the scarlet letter of *sandbagging,* otherwise known as cheating.

Beware the golfer who boasts of hitting a cell phone
230 yards. Keep phone on silent mode, use only
for emergencies.

CELL PHONE REDUX

It doesn't matter who you are. With cell phones, as with salad forks, you either know the etiquette or you don't, a lesson

Tour de France winner Lance Armstrong learned to his cha-grin. Lance and Jeff Garvey, chairman and executive director of the Lance Armstrong Foundation (created to help people "with, through, and beyond cancer"), happened to be playing the North Course of the prestigious Los Angeles Country Club. Lance brought along his cell phone. Imagine his surprise when his first round with a caddie also became the first round in which he was asked, albeit politely, to leave his cell phone in the locker room.

CHARITY EVENTS

There's hardly a charitable enterprise that hasn't discovered golf's value as a fund-raising vehicle. A golf outing is a prover-bial win-win situation, more fun than mailing a check and an opportunity to do some good and get out of the office, not to mention opening up additional networking channels. The events are often scrambles. Mulligans and extra putts may be available for additional donations.

Normally a solitary undertaking, golf now becomes a team effort. Pace of play in scrambles can be torturous. Main-taining a good pace is critical to making the experience enjoy-able. It's paramount to be ready to play when it's your turn. Cutting down on practice swings, not taking extra putts, not searching for lost balls, can make or break the experience.

Particularly in scrambles, newer golfers, if they can hit a good shot now and then, will find themselves treated almost royally. Inexperienced golfers in team competitions are given more strokes, which only means that when they do score a par or even a birdie, the team really cashes in. There are prizes to be won, but it's all in fun and benefits a worthy cause.

○ Were you playing on your own, standing directly behind a golfer would be a breach of etiquette, especially disconcerting on the green. In scrambles, however, it's common to have players line up behind a teammate putting.

There are seemingly no limits to how far charitable golf can go. The Shell Houston Open continues to raise millions of dollars for local charities, enlisting over four thousand volunteers each year. "You have to have a connection with the community," Steven Miller says. "It isn't just about a [favorable] date. It isn't just about the players. I think to be successful you have to find some way to connect and make it a community activity. That's what the Shell Houston Open is today. It's really a community event."

Q: How does underwriting the Shell Houston Open help your business?

Steven Miller: One of the key tenets of our business program, which we call our blueprint, is about being a top corporate citizen. We work here. We live here. We think it's essential to give back to the communities in which we work, and also to the nation as a whole.

TALKING POINTS

Among friends miscues such as inadvertent cell phone calls can take on a humorous aspect. Longtime golf buds in at least one regular weekly game fine each other every time someone's cell phone rings. The money's pooled to buy drinks after the round.

Golfers are notorious for being longwinded about their bad breaks, something Horace Hutchinson noted many, many years ago, when he wrote: "I do not remember having met a golfer who did not consider himself on the whole a remarkably unlucky one."

The situation can't have improved. Suffering in silence has

never been a golfing strong suit. Those eager to share their misery got a cool reception from the old Silver Scot, Tommy Armour. "Tell me all about your round," he'd say. "Start with the three-putt on eighteen." PGA Champion Dave Marr, once an assistant to Armour at the famed Winged Foot Country Club in New York, had his own way of gently disarming a member. He'd listen to the player describe shot by shot what happened on the first hole and then on the second hole. As the golfer was set to continue undeterred, Marr would stop him and ask: "Are we going to go all eighteen? If we are, I'm going to need a cart."

Bobby Jones once gently took wife Mary to task for asking a golfer how he'd played earlier in the day. Before the player had a chance to respond, Jones interjected. "Mary, if Joe had done well, he would have told you long ago." True enough. Maybe that's why Harvey Penick always used to say: "Tell me about your good shots." He, like Armour and Marr, just wanted to hear shorter stories.

GOOD CLUBS

Does equipment make the golfer? No, but a good set of pro-line clubs from any of the major manufacturers certainly won't embarrass in a situation where impressions count.

PACKING A DITTY BAG

One savvy business golf traveler of our acquaintance keeps a bag handy in hopes of a golf invitation materializing before meeting's end. He stuffs golf shoes, ball marker, divot tool, a sleeve of golf balls, business cards, a clean pair of socks, and some tees into a shoe bag. He figures golf clubs can always be procured at the last minute, but finding a clean pair of socks, his lucky ball marker, and favorite balls on the road in an instant can be iffy at best. Should the possibility of a round arise, he's ready.

BRIEFING

• Golf tells a lot about a person. Patience, temperament, respect for the rules and others, how they respond to adversity, uncertainty, challenge, all will be revealed. Would you want to do business with someone who's deliberately, even defiantly, careless and reckless on the golf course? Dress appropriately. Be early.

• An established handicap will be required to play in a typical country club member-guest event.

• Be certain a good shot is, in fact, a good shot before offering compliments.

• Remember the purpose of the round. It's business, not shooting a good score. Why win $2 to risk losing a $2 million account?

• Talk business when the client broaches the subject. Not as he's about to play, not as he's getting out of the cart sizing up the shot.

• Given a choice, don't wager. Or make it small. Pay off.

• As host, look after your guest's interests. Pick tees appropriately, keep it light and enjoyable. Make sure details are taken care of in advance, including the pairing. Try to avoid filling out the foursome with an unaffiliated golfer.

• As guest, accept financial arrangements graciously. Follow the host's lead. Let the host set the tone, from the driving range to the seriousness of the round to the bets. Leave cell phones behind. Accept gimmes graciously.

- Pick up when the hole has lost its fun.

- Practice the simple courtesies—helping to find balls, replacing divots, replacing the flagstick, gathering up clubs around the green, keeping up with the group in front, etc.

- "Modest in victory, generous in defeat."

- Whatever happens, be quick about it. No need to apologize. Play on.

> "A man's true colors will surface quicker in a five-dollar Nassau than in any other form of peacetime diversion I can name."
> —Grantland Rice

Relaxing at poolside at Barton Creek Resort.

12 RESORT GOLF

"It is one of the pleasures of golf that it is played in such pleasant places."
—Bernard Darwin, *The Golf Courses of the British Isles* (1910)

We can dream but it's highly unlikely any of us will ever play a few sets on center court at Wimbledon. Nor will we ever savor the thrill of coming up the dugout steps to take the field at Yankee Stadium. Golf, however, provides unparalleled opportunities in sport. Think of it, we can walk the same fairways, putt the same greens, face and stare down the same challenges that menace the game's immortals at spectacular championship venues around the world.

Resorts offer this vicarious great escape, the pleasure of experiencing the best work of premier course designers on the most revered addresses in golf. The Old Course at St. Andrews, Pebble Beach, Pinehurst, Turnberry—they await the moment when we can stand in the exact spot and say to ourselves, "This putt to win the Open."

Pleasing as these prospects most certainly are, the resort experience can be mildly unsettling to the uninitiated. To accentuate the positive in what should be a memorable experience, Steve Tremeer and Chip Gist, longtime resort executives, offer the following suggestions.

Tipping. Wait until the end of the day, Steve suggests. "It really ought to be at the conclusion of the experience."

"What people must understand," Chip adds, "is that a facility doesn't want you to feel like you need to always be going into your pocket." Keep in mind that valet tips will be shared. Three to five dollars is typical for those cleaning and stowing clubs, but there are no standards. And it's not like the gratuities figured in on a restaurant bill as a percentage. As elsewhere, tips should be based on service above, and beyond. One shouldn't feel obligated. It's a judgment call. Some private clubs prohibit tipping, and tips are never expected for golf instructors.

Be Punctual. Call ahead for directions. Once you are on resort property finding the course may still take some time, and you'll want all of it to prepare: to find the locker room, check in at the golf shop, hook up with friends, get your bag situated, loosen up, get a cart, drive to the range, hit some balls, find the starter, and, at long last, head to the first tee. Rushing has never been conducive to good golf. Leave yourself plenty of time, a half hour to an hour.

Enjoy Yourself. Both gentlemen advise guests to take advantage of the exceptional service resorts pride themselves in providing.

"When someone's on the road, they may be away from home, but they're going to someone's home," Chip notes. "The people at the resort are proud of it, and they want you, as a guest, to feel comfortable. Use the services that are there. Use the locker room."

Label Everything. Clubs, bags, and travel covers should be easily identified. Shaft labels for clubs, a tag on the bag, and a name tag on the travel cover can forestall trying locating a needle in a haystack. At many resorts, especially those with more than one golf course, clubs can move surprising distances. Often piled on the backs of small vehicles and shuffled around, they can log impressive miles going from bag room to cart to course to rooms (or condos). Anyone who has lost a club knows how much faster it can find its way home with a name on it.

Rental Clubs. Maybe dragging the equivalent weight of a corpse halfway across the country for one round of golf isn't your idea of a good time. Rental clubs may be available, but be sure to ask what kind. Expect to spend $30 to $50 per set. Balls not included.

(These days, with spikes having gone the way of the wood shaft, golf shoes may not even be required. Check first. A pair of tennis shoes may be acceptable. Whatever you wear, be sure to change your shoes in the locker room, not sitting in a cart.)

Buy the Yardage Book. It may be free, attached to the clip on the cart's steering wheel, or on sale in the pro shop. Either way, having one is worthwhile. They're a map, guide-book, and Cliff Notes all in one. They'll detail the holes, provide the color code used in identifying pin locations, share some of the course history, and point out bathroom locations and hazards. This may be the best $5 or $6 you spend that day. (Overseas they're called by the trade name "Stroke Saver.")

A Tee Time Means Balls Are in the Air. Fashionably late does not exist in golf. If three members of your group are present, accounted for, and ready to go, you will be expected to check in with the starter ten minutes before your tee time and ready to tee off on time. Your fourth will just have to join you out on the golf course. Resorts generally run groups at ten minute intervals, a very civilized spacing. The course will do its best to accommodate plot complications, but golfers are expected to hold up their end by not holding up others.

Foursomes Have the Right of Way. Those uneasy about playing with strangers should share their concerns in advance with the golf shop or concierge. Otherwise, expect to be paired up. "The more information a resort has," Chip advises, "the better they can go out of their way to accommodate you. Otherwise, it's the luck of the draw. You may get paired with two scratch golfers." To which Steve hastens to add: "I'd rather play with a 40-handicap player in four hours than with a scratch golfer in five." Once again, it's not how good you are but how good you are to play with.

Stow Valuables in a Pouch. At the end of the day, golf bags find their way to a common bag room that closes with nightfall. Locating a bag after hours, when the room is filled with a hundred or more golf bags, will likely require above-and-beyond service and necessitate "something extra." Having everything together in a pouch will make it easier to remember your wallet, jewelry, Rolex, phone, etc. Taking the pouch out to tip at the end of the round is a good time to restore watches to wrists, rings to fingers, and wallets to pockets.

There's No Such Thing As a Stupid Question. Curious what's on the beverage cart? Want to arrange a lesson for a non-golfing spouse during your round? Can lunch at the halfway house be charged back to the room? Ask. If you don't, both the guest and the staff will be uncomfortable. Staff is trained to take care of every golfer in the same way, from the best to the newest, but they need to know what's on your mind.

Taking Home a Souvenir? Postpone shopping until after the round so there will be one less thing to lose and shopping won't delay the tee time. Check to make sure the golf shop won't be closed by the time you finish so you won't miss the opportunity.

Drop the Resort a Note. Was anything outstanding? What could be improved? Resorts that value customer service very much want to know where they have succeeded and where they need work.

GOLF IN THE BRITISH ISLES

Playing across the Atlantic is an exhilarating experience, but it is different. It helps to know how things are done in Rome, as in "when in . . ." Many of the older clubs, for instance, require *smarter* dress for lunch in the clubhouse. A fine line separates a well-meant caddie tip from an affront.

Scotsman Gordon Dalgleish is president of luxury golf travel companies Perry Golf and Intergolf Vacations, based in Atlanta. A very good golfer, he's also an old hand at helping Americans savor what for many truly is the trip of a lifetime. He shares several thoughts for those contemplating the pilgrimage.

Americans occasionally bristle at policies that strike us as restrictive or even snobbish.

"I was talking to a chap yesterday," Gordon recalls, "about a course that he thought was rather stuffy. This course in particular, Muirfield, requires members and visitors alike to put on a jacket and tie to go in to lunch. And that's just part of their process and the whole experience. And his view was that it was rather a stuffy environment and that they weren't particularly welcoming to visitors.

"But the other way to look at it is that here you've got one of the best courses and most exclusive clubs in the British Isles and they allow visitors to come and enjoy their facilities, albeit under their rules. Now, if you were to reverse that situation to the United States, the better clubs for the most part do not allow visitor play unless you are the guest of a member, either accompanied or unaccompanied. So the better clubs in the British Isles really do encourage people to enjoy the facilities, but under their rules. And that's one of the things that people don't think about."

Practice swings, Gordon says, can also be a source of misunderstanding. Americans are often admonished for taking them on the first tee. Some courses post signs prohibiting them. What's up with that?

"It's something that's kind of accepted in the U.S.—the guys warming up," Gordon explains, "but in Scotland and Ireland it takes so long for the grass to grow—the season is so short—the view is: Why damage the tee when you can go and stand to the side and practice your swing before you start?

"And Americans think that it's rude of the starter to chase them from the first tee for practice-swinging but it's just to protect the golf course. That's one thing that people from Britain are very respectful of, the golf course and maintaining it, because it's such an integral part of the lifestyle over there."

That's definitely one of its charms. Everyone, it seems, plays golf, and in Scotland that's been the case for centuries. Another policy that can be misconstrued concerns visitors not being allowed to play the back tees. It's not a slight, Gordon points out. Nor is it that for many visitors; the championship tees would be inappropriate.

"I grew up in Scotland, and you always played the one set

of tees," he said, "the regular tees. You never had a choice, even the better players. The back tees were kept for club competitions. It's only reasonable that if the members can't use the back tees during normal play that visitors don't use the back tees. It's sometimes a sore point with Americans who are visiting, but again it's the overall maintenance of the golf course, and if everybody played the back tees all the time, they'd be pretty well beaten up for the members' competition. So again, it's the respectful approach."

That underpinning of respect carries well beyond the golf course, as many Americans discover. (Pssst: Remove that hat or ball cap indoors.)

"When you meet somebody and you're shaking hands at the end of a golf game or before you play, or whenever," says Gordon, "the respectful thing to do is to take your hat off. In the same way that when a lady comes to the table, you get up and help her sit down."

Walking into the clubhouse as a lad without remembering, he says, would get him "a quick slap across the head. I know the cap is part of the lifestyle [in the U.S.]. I think it just may be more of the European upbringing [to take it off]. It just looks a little bit more respectful, a little bit better."

Tipping caddies, always a concern, can be ticklish:

"The total remuneration generally seems to be in the £40 a bag range," says Gordon, "which is inclusive of a tip. Quite honestly, caddie pricing is one thing I've never been able to understand fully, because if you work on a percentage basis from a base figure, the caddie fee might be posted as £20 or £25 but the market seems to have gotten the total up to maybe £40 or a number like that, £35 to £40, which doesn't hold any percentage relationship to the base. If you're using a number like £35 to £40 you're not going to embarrass yourself or make the caddie feel he's been shortchanged. And they will certainly make their feelings known without much hesitation."

As of the summer of 2002, £30, tip included, was just about right. As long as everyone in the group tips the same, there shouldn't be too much grumbling.

On the experience of playing in Scotland, Ireland, England, and Wales more from Gordon:

> The golf over there is just so different than it is here, the whole experience. And I think that's one of the things that Americans enjoy so much—to get over there and get into the pubs and interface with the caddies and tell stories and enjoy maybe just a little bit more relaxed lifestyle than they engage in in the United States.

On trying to do too much:

> I think that's a common mistake. As much as you try to encourage people to think about it rationally, they just want to play as much golf and see as many of the golf courses, but the reality is the courses will be there next year and the year after. And I think it makes more sense, it's more enjoyable, to maybe only stay in two hotels and play some of the golf courses twice. Don't play thirty-six holes everyday. You might take a few days, play eighteen and enjoy the countryside and the pubs and you're not rushing around.
>
> I've seen any number of groups of guys who will play twelve rounds of golf in seven days and as a result they have to stay in five different hotels. It's such an oppressive schedule to keep and at the end of it, one golf course will run into the next in terms of your memory. I think you're better served to play five courses and maybe you play a couple of them twice. You stay in two hotels and you've got some great memories. You remember what the golf courses are all about.

On what women can expect:

Britain is remarkably evenhanded. There are obviously some famous occasions where ladies aren't particularly welcome in clubhouses, which is unfortunate, but for the most part ladies are welcome at the golf course over there. There are ladies' tees on the courses. They'll be treated as well as men. Asking a club official where, for instance, a woman golfer can get a beverage or lunch will ameliorate any possible misstep. You'll be steered to the proper place.

And, finally, what about mixing scotch with water—neat or on the side?

I think you've got to keep it unsullied with water, and keep those ice cubes out of it as well.

BRIEFING:

- Tip after the round. Three to five dollars is standard for those cleaning and stowing clubs. You needn't feel obligated or nickel and dimed.
- Avail yourself of the facilities. Use the locker room. Enjoy yourself.
- Leave time to stretch, find your way around, hook up with friends. Call for directions.
- Find out not only *if* rental clubs are available but what kind.
- Label your clubs and travel cover. Have a tag on your bag.
- Yardage books may be the best $5 you spend that day.
- Tee times mean balls are in the air.
- Foursomes have the right of way. Share concerns with the golf shop or concierge.

- There's no such thing as an inappropriate question.
- Play now, shop later—after the round.

> "Progress, I should warn you, comes in stages. It is rather like climbing a ladder. You gain one rung, then slip back two, then gain three and think what a clever fellow you are—this being the moment when for a certainty you slip back two again."
>
> —Henry Longhurst, *How to Get Started in Golf*

Everything in its place. Putter and woods together in the top slot, irons paired together on the sides, wedges in the bottom slot.

13   EQUIPMENT

"To the player who is in the throes of inca-
pacity with a certain club, a new implement
is ethereal; it holds out unbounded promise."
—Harry Vardon, *How to Play Golf* (1913)

While not strictly an etiquette concern, golf equipment presents another rite of passage. There's just not a book on how to
buy golf stuff; it'd be too boring anyway. It has been noted
that golfers are the only demographic category that actually
enjoys reading the ads.

It's no surprise then, given the addicting nature of the
game, that golf equipment has a way of finding and latch ing
onto golfers, eventually filling basements, trunks, and garages.
Good equipment makes a world of difference. *The two most
important keys to learning and enjoying golf are investing in
better equipment and getting qualified instruction.*

WHERE TO BUY GOLF CLUBS

Golf shops, off-course golf retail stores, and Internet sites will
have the largest selection. Sporting goods stores don't specialize in golf and are not recommended for clubs, but they are a

good source for minor purchases: balls, tees, bags, and gloves. Always carefully consider warranty and return policies before buying online.

DIFFERENT OPTIONS

Purchasing clubs is a daunting task complicated by an abundance of information, good intentions, a ferociously competitive marketplace, and hype. We strongly feel that following the old saying "Buy something cheap until you learn how to play" is ill-advised. Golf is difficult enough to master with top-of-the-line clubs. The better the equipment, the easier it is to use. Nothing revelatory perhaps, but if you doubt us, try training for a marathon in a $19 pair of sneakers.

Golf equipment falls into four categories:

1. Pro-line
   Sold in pro shops and off-course golf retail shops. Top-of-the-line in quality and price. Also known as OEM (for Original Equipment Manufacturer—of name-brand equipment).
2. Store-line
   Sold in department, discount chain, and sporting goods stores. Adding to the confusion, some manufacturers put the name *pro* on their clubs, as in "pro star" or "pro play," to imply they are pro-line. Lesser quality materials are used in lower-priced models.
3. Component clubs
   Will not have the benefits of computer technology with respect to playing characteristics such as weight, balance, or consistency as compared to pro-line clubs. The parts are sold separately: grips, shafts, and heads, and then assembled locally.

4. Knock-offs

Illegal copies of pro-line clubs. Often similar in name to popular pro-line equipment and sold at a fraction of the price.

BUYING CLUBS

Adding to the confusion, several of the larger golf equipment manufacturers make clubs for both the pro-line and store-line markets. The fine print of club specifications, if we could decipher it, would note that materials of lesser quality and lower standards are used in the production of the less expensive models. Basically, you get what you pay for. *New players will especially benefit from better clubs because of the inconsistent nature of their swings.* Better clubs tend to be more "forgiving" (better shots even when not struck perfectly). Starting out, center your search on finding a high-quality, used set of name-brand clubs. Golfers are notoriously fickle. Many upgrade with the change of season (and new ad campaigns). Driven by demand, equipment continues to evolve and improve (and go up in price). Few can keep up with it. Golf club manufacturing may not be rocket science, but the engineering effort expanded to improve golf performance, even by modest increments, rivals NASA's.

Much is often made of the expense involved in taking up the game, but acquiring a ball and putter surely won't break the bank. Putting and chipping, imperative to playing well, are not expensive pastimes. Public courses allow the practice of these important skills anytime, without a reservation, for free. And good used clubs are readily available. Major championships have been won with used putters.

○ You can often find a high-quality used set cheaper than a new low-quality set.

PRO-LINE EQUIPMENT

We recommend it because the manufacturing standards are so much higher; more attention is paid (and more money spent) on detail and performance. Purchasing a new set of golf clubs is like buying any other high-ticket item these days. If it seems that the price of a top-of-the-line set of golf clubs rivals the cost of a major home appliance, that's only because a ravenous public insists on ever better equipment. And just like cars, known brands have better *Blue Book* value. Golf clubs depreciate the moment they leave the store on their way to the garage or classified section of Sunday's paper.

OEM clubs will retain their value longer, for up to ten years. A good set of clubs can be amortized over several years. Think of having a set for five or six years. The quality of the investment will get you over the initial sticker shock.

○ Buying tip: Pro-line clubs can often be purchased at close-out and end-of-season sales before new models are introduced, typically in the spring, the start of traditional golf season.

BUYING ONE A CLUB AT A TIME

Every year new clubs replace last year's model. A partial set of irons, unlikely to ever be completed, will have limited lasting value. A better purchase would be a used set of pro-line irons no more than five years old. Store-line clubs and component clubs have limited sale or trade-in value.

It is OK to buy just one wood to start, preferably a three- or five-wood. Golfers often mix and match woods of different makes, but not irons, which are sold in sets.

USED CLUBS AND "STARTER" SETS

Let's suppose an ad in Sunday's classified section catches your eye. A golf bag, ten irons, four woods, and a putter, asking price $100. Sounds like a deal. But you saw a set of used name-brand irons in a golf store for $250. No bag, no putter, no woods, the irons alone cost over twice as much. What gives? Which is ultimately the better deal? Well, Monty, difficult as that first package may be to pass up, remember the admonitions on quality instead of quantity. When buying used clubs from want ads or over the Internet, focus on a well-known brand name and the shaft flex (discussed later in the chapter). A golf shop or golf specialty store can help determine a set's value. There are even shops that specialize in good used equipment.

Beginning golfers are often steered to so-called starter sets. It's no surprise many never progress in the game. With starter sets the cards are stacked against them. The quality is simply inferior, and golf is hard enough without inferior equipment.

Many courses, in conjunction with club manufacturers, offer Demo Days. It's an opportunity to take clubs out for a test drive. You won't be able to hit the exact club you'll purchase, but you will be able to sample a wide variety of equipment, for free, in a short period of time. We recommend hitting clubs before making a purchase, even if it's just into a net.

Pay close attention to a club's shaft flex and length.

CLUBS OFF THE RACK

All those but the very tall or very short can buy clubs right off the rack. Custom fitting can be a valuable tool, given a skilled and experienced "tailor." It can also help narrow the choices, but it's certainly not imperative.

An important consideration, regardless of manufacturer or budget considerations, is shaft *flex,* its flexibility. The firmer the shaft, the more speed it takes to solidly strike the ball. Not all of us generate the same speed swinging a golf club. The pros top out at over 120 mph. That's a tremendous amount of force brought to bear. Many of us, however, never reach 80 mph. *Determining proper shaft flex is critical to finding enjoyable clubs.* Clubs passed down or given as gifts often have an incorrect shaft flex.

Customers at Empowered Women's Golf go through an extensive interview to find the right clubs, a process that can take hours. We're delighted to pass along owner Patricia Dixon's expertise on shafts. Note that trade names differ widely. While the buzzwords may change, the bottom line for man or woman, beginner or expert, remains marrying the right shaft to the proper swing speed. Here are Patricia's recommendations:

Flex is graded by the manufacturer in five general categories.

From most flexible to least flexible, those flexes are L (or women's), A (or seniors), R (regular), S (stiff), and XS (extra stiff). Different manufacturers may call the flexes by special names such as "light flex" or "moderate swing speed," but in the industry, they are known as L, A, R, S, XS. The right flex for you is the one that flexes enough but not too much. A club that is too stiff for you will create an arc that is very low and a ball that generally goes right. A club that is too flexible for you will "spray" the ball—go up too high, go right sometimes, go left sometimes, and generally create such inconsistency that you cannot depend on the result.

Clubs flex at a particular spot on the shaft. A good quality shaft will have a very consistent flex point that will result in a feeling that is the same for each club in your set and will remain the same no matter how many times you hit it. If the club flexes very low, or close to the head, you will probably feel that is more flexible than one that flexes higher up the shaft. You may describe that feeling as being "easier" to swing. A mid or high flex (or "kick point") may feel more solid with higher swing speeds, but that is not usually appropriate for amateurs.

Men typically play clubs with a regular flex shaft. Men with slower swing speeds, craving more distance with less effort, will benefit from an A flex shaft. Pros, with speed to burn, typically chose an extra stiff shaft, one that hardly bends at all during the swing.

Another shaft consideration is the choice between steel or graphite. Graphite is lighter and better at absorbing shock. Those bothered by wrist, elbow, neck, or back ailments gravitate to it. Lighter than steel, a selling point in generating distance (always in demand), it's considered more forgiving, placing less stress on the joints.

Newcomers need only be concerned with the shaft's flex and length and whether they have a preference for graphite over steel. Graphite shafts are more expensive but will likely last a lifetime.

WOMEN'S CLUBS

Aspiring women golfers, including the salespeople waiting on them, often don't realize that clubs made expressly for women are approximately an inch shorter than standard men's clubs. Women five foot five and up should consider "men's" clubs with an A or senior shaft. They'll get the length they need swinging the longer club wedded to the proper shaft. Buy graphite shafts. With a lighter shaft, the clubhead is heavier. It makes it easier to swing and generate more speed, which makes it easier to get the ball up in the air and go farther. Taller women are often mistakenly sold shorter clubs, even in pro shops, by well-meaning professionals unfamiliar with women's equipment.

Husbands or significant others who purchase clubs as gifts often don't know the difference. Many women end up leaving golf little knowing they've been betrayed by ill-fitting equipment. Men, because of their strength, can occasionally make up for lesser quality, but women shouldn't be placed at a disadvantage, nor should they have to pay for it.

BUYING A PUTTER

A putter should be a golfer's first purchase. With a near-infinite number of styles and price points, from mallets to blades, from $30 to $300, the deciding factors are personal preference and cost. It's the violinist, not the violin, that determines success with the flat stick. The putter is the one club that can be passed from one golfer to the next or shared without the problems associated with irons (length, weight, shaft flex, etc.). Many of the materials used in putters, aluminum and brass, to name two, are just as desirable today as they were a hundred years ago.

PETRIFIED WOODS

Once made from persimmon and other hardwoods, modern woods are in fact constructed from blended metal alloys. These distance clubs need not match your irons. Golfers mix and match brands all the time. The first wood purchase should be a 3-wood, versatile and easier to hit than a driver. Add a 5- or 7-wood and lastly the driver, also called the 1-wood. The 9- and 11-woods are also popular options. Every now and then a golfer or announcer will refer to them as "metals," but old traditions die hard in golf. Most still call them woods.

WEDGES

A well-struck wedge quickly gets the ball up in the air and stops it on the green with hardly any roll. If you can only afford one—they can be bought separately, like putters—get a sand wedge first. It can be used from bunkers or from short range in the fairway. A pitching wedge is for longer distances and isn't as serviceable from sand. For skilled players, a "gap" wedge fills the precise distance requirements between the sand

and pitching wedges. A "lob" wedge is for shorter perilous shots, when the ball must rise quickly and land softly.

BALLS

They're all round and the same size, but golf balls come in dizzying varieties, from dimple shape and number to what's inside to their alleged properties (better for putting, better for driving, better for everything!). Naturally they also differ in price. Barbara always gets a laugh when students ask what ball she recommends. It's almost impossible these days for anyone to keep up with the parade of new models and performance claims, so she recommends round. That's it. Not this core or that compression, this cover or that brand, just round. Manufacturing is so good now that any ball that makes it to market is going to be excellent. "X-outs," so called because of cosmetic flaws, are also a good buy. Typically discounted, these new balls are the result of canceled orders or printing errors. The ball itself is sound.

Buying balls is a bit like buying tires. High performance tires for sports cars are more expensive and probably won't last as long as tires for your SUV. Whichever brand you choose, new balls are best. Used balls, the ones on the pro shop counter, may have a checkered past—fished out of water hazards, for instance, and repainted. A waterlogged ball will certainly not perform well, never mind that it looks like all the rest and is much cheaper. (As you'll discover, for good reason.)

Manufacturers will tell you that certain balls are customized to general playing characteristics. Frankly, the ball may be lost long before its playing capabilities diminish. Better players over time do develop loyalties and perhaps even sensitivities to one over another. It all boils down to personal preference. Most of us can get along quite happily with round.

"There can be no doubt about the 'Eclipse' being the better ball to play with against the wind; it also retains its roundness, a great desideratum in putting, and is the most economical ball."
—*Newcastle Daily Journal*, April 14, 1887

HAND IN GLOVE

Right-handed golfers wear a glove on the left hand; left-handed golfers wear one on their right hand. In each case it's the hand that first grips the club. Don't fret should the wrong one be purchased by mistake. Hold on to it. In cold weather, it will make a perfect match and keep hands warm.

BAGS

Should you walk, or travel, weight should be the major consideration in selecting a bag. Get something lightweight. You'll also need a sturdy travel cover, a requirement of the airlines and prudent protection for your investment.

WHAT YOU NEED

- Balls
- Tees
- Divot repair tool
- Glove
- Ball marks

WHAT YOU MAY NEED

- Sunscreen
- Insect repellent

WHAT YOU DON'T NEED

- Rubber or fur-lined individual iron covers.
- Plastic tube shaft protectors.
- Swing gimmicks pitched on infomercials (invest instead in a lesson).
- Any of a 1,001 doodads to hold balls, scorecards, or tees.

ARRANGING CLUBS IN YOUR BAG

The pros are very fastidious. Sneak a peek in their bags and you'll find everything just so. The woods are in the top slot along with the putter. ("Top" meaning closest to the strap. On a bag with a tripod stand, it's the tallest slot.) The two side-by-side slots hold neighboring irons, for instance: the 5- and 6-irons together, the 7- and 8-irons together. The bottom slot is for wedges, pitching and sand (and, for some, lob or gap), and the 9-iron. Nothing to it. A sense of order is helpful out on the golf course. With a slot for each club, it's easier to keep track of them and not leave one behind. Now, if you can just remember which bag pocket has the car keys without tearing everything apart.

BRIEFING

- Concentrate on pro-line clubs, even used, with the appropriate shaft. Avoid starter sets.

- The better the equipment, the easier it is to play with. The better the equipment, the faster the progress.

- What kind of ball should you play? "Round." Balls will be lost long before the playing characteristics wane. X-outs are a good buy.

● Woods go in the bag in the top slot with the putter, wedges on the bottom.

> "It's good sportsmanship not to pick up lost golf balls while they are still rolling." —Mark Twain

Legendary teacher Harvey Penick (left) hard at work.
Photo courtesy of *Texas Golfer* magazine.

14 TAKING LESSONS

"There has been criticism that some professional golfers do not know how to teach. In defense of my competent colleagues in professional golf, I must point out that many pupils don't know how to take a lesson."
—Tommy Armour, *A Round of Golf with Tommy Armour*

There's not an accomplished golfer who hasn't benefited by instruction. The best players in the world routinely take lessons. With the pros it may be more like fine-tuning a high-performance engine than building from the ground up, but no one is born with a golf swing.

Swing instruction is beyond the scope of this book, but the process of learning golf presents another series of social hurdles that clearly influences one's impression of golf and the decision to stay with it. The following guidelines are offered for those who may feel confused, not only in learning golf but in knowing where to start and how to proceed.

HOW TO FIND A PRO

A good golf teaching pro is found the same way one finds a reputable plumber or painter: word of mouth. Ask around. Personalities and teaching styles vary. *The best tip you ever get may be the one that leads you to a skilled teacher and communicator, not just a good player, but someone with a good record in helping others.* They may be based at a course or a driving range. Good teachers can be found just about anywhere golf is played.

QUESTIONS THE GOLF PRO SHOULD ASK BEFORE THE LESSON

How long have you played?

How often do you play?

What is your handicap or average score?

Do you practice? How often?

Be sure to mention any physical problems that might have a bearing on your ability to proceed—tendonitis, past injuries or surgeries, etc.

If he or she doesn't ask, volunteer the information. The pro should also be interested in your motivation and expectations. Be honest, if you've never played before, say so. None of this is going on your permanent record. What the pro really wants to know is what's happening to the ball when you hit it. "It goes to the right most of the time." "I'm hitting the top of it." "I'm missing it completely." "My drives are popping up." "My swing is inhabited by demon spirits."

You needn't feel embarrassed in front of the instructor. The reason you're taking lessons is to avoid looking silly on the golf course in front of friends or business associates. This is the time to address and straighten out problems.

WHAT THE GOLF PRO DOESN'T WANT TO HEAR

"My right elbow is flying."

"My hips spin too fast."

"I'm swinging too far back." Or, "I'm not swinging long enough."

"My husband says I'm not keeping my head down and my left arm straight."

Symptoms are one thing, effecting a cure is another. Leave the swing analysis and diagnosis to the expert. To the above list we might also add:

- Exclamations of disappointment after every shot.
- Tips from friends and relatives.
- Explanations of what went wrong ("I took my eye off that one." "I swayed on that one." "I was too fast.")
- "That feels funny."

It's perfectly OK to bring up a previous session with another pro. Seeking second opinions is not uncommon. Frankly, golf pros are in an enviable position. Swing problems remain an epidemic. When improvement doesn't happen, students blame themselves. If results with one instructor are not satisfactory, find another. And beware of the teacher who hits a lot of balls during a lesson to impress students. A good "bedside" manner, experience, competence, convenience, reasonable price—that's what you want. After all, you're buying. Inexperienced golfers are often shunted off to inexperienced teachers. You want someone who knows what he's doing. Ask questions. Get your money's worth.

Harvey Penick had this suggestion about lessons for established players: Have one bad day, forget about it. We all have them. Have two bad days, go to the range and try and work it out. Have three bad days, seek help from a pro. Invariably, new instruction will feel different, weird, uncomfortable. Give it a chance. Reverting back to what feels "comfortable" will only lead right back to the old, unsatisfactory, results.

"I think I am going to start teaching like the weatherman. One has a 20 percent chance of hitting a good shot, or a 40 percent or a 50 percent chance. I sometimes think I, and some other golfers, have an upper level disturbance."

—Harvey Penick

Group lessons are great for beginning golfers. The brain can only absorb so much, and watching others speeds the learning process. They offer an opportunity to observe and practice without someone standing behind on every shot. Plus, they're more fun. Golf's a social game. Starting out in a group lightens the air. It also introduces potential friends and playing partners. Group lessons are also less expensive. A visit to a golf school can also be a vacation, and a few days of intense concentration on the game that wouldn't happen at home. Many schools are held at premier resorts.

Video lessons, a popular teaching tool, are a tremendous teaching aid in conveying the proper movements of the swing, but the swing is still yours to make. Identifying flaws on tape is one thing, correcting them something else. Video provides an insight into the elements of a good swing. It is particularly helpful to the experienced player, but still fun for the newcomer to watch.

WHAT TO BRING TO A LESSON

Golf clubs may or may not be provided. In group lessons for beginners they often are. Wear golf shoes or sneakers. We asked several teachers, among the game's most widely recognized and respected, what they like to see students bring to a lesson, not in the way of equipment, but with respect to creating a climate conducive to improvement.

A PGA Tour fixture, David Leadbetter relies on the student to fill in many of the blanks:

> No matter what the level of player, I think you look first at thinking in terms of "what is this person's goal?" I mean, some people don't have great goals. All they want to do is go out and enjoy themselves. Maybe a wife just wants to get good enough to play with her husband. And that's fine. It's a matter, really, of taking into account: talent level, the time they've got to put into it, and really what they want to do. If they want to do it, with good instruction, it's amazing how far you can go. It does really depend on what the player, what the person, wants.

He also ticked off these qualities: "Enthusiasm, an open mind, and a willingness to work at it. That's really what it takes. Then I think it's just a meeting of the minds between the teacher and the player."

Tina Bradley, a gifted instructor following in the footsteps of her father, Texas legend Jackson Bradley, recalls the difficulty of learning a musical instrument.

> I find it's always easier to teach someone who doesn't expect to master the game in an hour. A relaxed attitude often brings success about quicker. Of course it's easier when the student has some athletic ability. Setting realistic goals is important when learning anything new. I remember when I tried to learn to play

the guitar—I discovered quickly that if I didn't practice frequently, my instructor just gave me the same lesson over and over. If the student understands that building a golf swing is a process, similar to building a house, the journey is much easier for both of us.

Bryan Gathright, *Golf* magazine top 100 teacher, echoes David's point about establishing and meeting student expectations.

The practice schedule and time the student has available for golf has to match their expectations and goals. I think it's very important to establish that right from the beginning in the first lesson, to see that those expectations and goals match up to what they have time to accomplish. That's a major problem that I see a lot—that they don't have time to do that. Secondly, once you've established that, you've got to show them that you have a game plan for them, and that progress and change do take time.

Nothing's magical. You have to work through and show them how to work toward the common goal that you and that person put together. The other thing I encourage players, is not to get away from playing the game. Even though the swing may get better, you still have to remember how to play and how to go out there and dig a round out.

Dave Pelz, a former NASA scientist who's dedicated his life to researching and teaching the so-called short game (100 yards and in to the green, including putting), emphasizes the importance of attitude.

A "can do" attitude is really the key. I like to see students come into a lesson with the idea that "I can learn anything if you can show me how to do it properly and explain it in a way that I'll understand." It also helps if they have a strong desire to improve—if they want it bad enough and they're willing to practice, they really can improve. It's the students who are willing to invest time in practicing the proper techniques beyond their initial instruction who will really get the most out of it. But they have to come in with that willingness and commitment.

Chuck Cook, a past PGA Teacher of the Year, echoes the point:

The success of a golf lesson for a beginning golfer or a touring golf professional is determined by the student's attitude. The willingness to try something new or the acceptance of change makes the lesson a positive experience for student and instructor.

Finally, Hank Haney, another member of golf's teaching elite, stresses that how "good" a golfer is doesn't matter. "I have no preference as to someone's ability level, my only wish," he responded, "is for someone with a good positive attitude and realistic expectations."

BRIEFING

Some perspective

- There are 26.7 million golfers in the United States.
- 6.3 million play 25 rounds a year or more.
- The average male golfer's score is 97.
- The average female golfer's score is 114.
- Six percent of male golfers break 80 on a regular basis.
- One percent of ladies break 80.
- Twenty-five percent of men break 90.
- Seven percent of women break 90.

Source: National Golf Foundation

"Amateurs teach amateurs, professionals teach golfers."
—Anonymous

"Parents often ask me how best they can help their children to become proficient at the game, how to encourage them, how to guide them. I was given my love for the game and my first lessons—very good lessons too—by my parents, particularly my father. What I am most grateful for, though I was not at the time—I thought he was being hard—was that as soon as I began to play my father insisted that I should be conversant with the etiquette of the game. He drilled it into me that when you are playing golf a constant thought in your mind must be consideration for other people on the course."
—*Bobby Locke on Golf* (1954)

A QUICK DEFINITION
OF TERMS

Golf has a colorful language; fluency comes with experience. There are, however, a few key terms to learn to allow one to feel more a part of the game.

THE SWING AND WHAT HAPPENS NEXT

fat, thin Like Eskimos, who have many words to describe snow, golfers have umpteen ways of describing shots. A fat shot takes too much turf and lands well short of its target. Its cousin, commonly played around the green, is the **chili dip,** the chip shot that needs to go forty feet but only goes three when the club stubs in the ground. A thin shot catches the ball above its center, also missing the sweet spot.

skulled, topped Catches the very top of the ball and rolls it along the ground; it often goes as far as a shot hit well in the air. It isn't pretty but can be satisfactory. Also known as a "wormburner."

short/long, upright/flat, fast/slow Terse descriptions of swings, as individual as a thumbprint: short and long refer to the length of a golfer's backswing; fast and slow to its speed. A flat swing moves more horizontally around the body instead of being lifted more upright.

whiff, fan Awful as it may be to swing at the ball and miss, the whiff only counts one stroke. A ball hit into the water or out of bounds causes us to be playing our third shot, not our second.

lay up The prudent strategy of deliberately playing short, for instance, of a hazard rather than risk hitting into it. By *laying up*, the next shot will be less taxing.

WHAT THE BALL DOES (FOR RIGHT-HANDERS)

hook A ball that veers sharply to the left.

draw A ball that in flight turns slightly to the left.

slice A ball that veers sharply to the right.

fade A ball that in flight bends slightly to the right. A fade doesn't roll as far as a shot hit with a draw but is a shot that is under control.

push A push starts out to the right and stays fairly straight.

pull A pull starts out to the left and stays fairly straight.

shank A sideways shot so horrific some golfers can't even say the word.

sky An undesirable shot that goes too high; same as *popped-up*.

carry How far a ball flies in the air.

run How far it rolls along the ground.

chip A low-trajectory shot that has more ground time than air time.

pitch A higher-trajectory shot that has more air time than ground time.

THE GOLF CLUB

hosel The neck of the club into which the shaft is attached to the head.

face Which meets the ball.

head Attaches to the shaft and strikes the ball.

toe Like the toe of your foot, farthest forward from where the club meets the shaft.

heel The opposite of the toe.

sole The bottom edge of the club that touches the ground.

THE GOLF COURSE

blind A *blind* hole requires a shot on faith; the golfer will not be able to see where the ball lands. Playing to a green at the top of a steep hill would require a *blind* shot.

dogleg An obscure anatomical reference, a hole that bends to the left or right, typically about halfway between the tee and the green. Were we to look at it from above, the fairway would appear to bend.

apron, collar, fringe All mean the same thing: the grass edge just off the putting green.

first cut, second cut Ways of describing the area off the fairway; also called primary and secondary. The first cut is just off the fairway; the second cut is the deep rough.

SCORING

ace A hole-in-one.

double-eagle At least as rare, scoring a 2 on a par-5 hole.

eagle Scoring two under par, a 3 on a par-5 hole, for example.

birdie Cause for celebration, scoring one under par: a 2 on a par 3, a 3 on a par 4, a 4 on a par 5.

par Once considered perfect golf, scoring the suggested number of strokes on a hole.

bogey One over par, a 5 on a par 4.

double-bogey Two over par, a 7 on a par 5.

triple-bogey An "other," or whatever you want to call it: three over par.

ETCETERA

shotgun start In tournaments, teams start on each hole rather than all beginning at the first. Saves time, and the field finishes at approximately the same time.

winter rules Informal leniency commonly invoked by recreational golfers when poor conditions merit it. Winter rules allow golfers to roll or move their ball into a better position, typically within a club length of where the ball lands.

summer rules The ball is played "down," as it lies, from wherever it lands.

BETTER PLAYERS

- Expect nothing more than timely play and proper etiquette.

- Wince when they hear "Nice par" when it's really a bogey or a birdie.

- Don't want to be told "Good shot" when they merely get the ball airborne.

- Don't exactly relish listening to a litany of weaknesses: how you'll ruin their game, slow them down, or how seldom or poorly you play.

- Aren't bothered if you improve your lie in the fairway, as long as it keeps play moving *except* during a tournament when, in fairness to the field, everyone plays by the same rules.

- Would do well to remember that they too were once new to the game.

- Will be grateful should you pick up when the hole has lost its fun or when you've fallen behind.

- Need to remember their responsibility to play in a timely manner.

NEW GOLFERS

- Appreciate the interest but don't want an on-course lesson.

- Most definitely want to be treated as equals, afforded the same courtesies as better players, even when playing from the forward tees.

- Would love to be recognized with a "Nice par" when they make one.

- Wish better players wouldn't repeatedly drive past their tee box before they've played.

- Would like to be asked before their putts are kicked back as gimmes.

- Have trouble being sympathetic to those disappointed with shots that would thrill us.

- Appreciate playing with better golfers, and are nervous doing so.

- Recognize that playing in a timely manner has little to do with skill.

GOLF ETIQUETTE'S 10 *LEAST* WANTED LIST

1. Not being ready to play.

2. Mulligans.

3. Stepping on putting lines.

4. Unsolicited advice.

5. Too many practice swings.

6. Ignoring divots and pitch marks.

7. Cell phones.

8. Stage whispers.

9. Neglected bunkers.

10. Jingling coins (for men).

COMMENCEMENT ADDRESS

Congratulations, graduates. With your Doctorate in Continuous Dealing (D.C.D.), you are now free to confidently step up to the first tee and pursue your ambitions in your chosen field with golf as a valuable asset. As you make your way in the world, availing yourself of business golf opportunities around the globe, we, those who already play and love the game, welcome you in your resolve to play in a timely manner, to respect the rules of competition in fairness to the field, to begin and end your round with a handshake, to purposefully practice the customs of sportsmanship so meaningful to golf, and to never lose sight of both the fairway and your client's golfing comfort level. We send you on your way, then, ladies and gentleman, as you close this important chapter, with the hope that you will not be one of those endlessly moaning sad sacks crowding the 19th hole, but an observant, considerate golfer who continues to strive, not just to be good, but to be good to play with. Never forget the reminder of the legendary Harvey Penick: "Playing golf is a privilege, not a sentence." Give yourself a round of applause. (Cue to "Pomp and Circumstance.")

READING LIST

Armour, Thomas D. *A Round of Golf with Tommy Armour.*
Bauer, Aleck. *Hazards.*
Chapman, Kenneth G. *The Rules of the Green.*
Concannon, Dale, comp. *Wise Words for Golfers.*
The Darrell Survey. *Golf Equipment Almanac, 2000.*
Henderson, Ian T., and David I. Stirk. *Golf in the Making.*
Jarman, Colin M., ed. *The Hole Is More Than the Sum of the Putts.*
Jones, Robert Tyre, Jr. *Bobby Jones on Golf.*
Jones, Robert Trent, Jr. *Golf by Design.*
Leonard, Terry, ed. *In the Women's Clubhouse.*
Locke, Bobby. *Bobby Locke on Golf.*
Longhurst, Henry. *How to Get Started in Golf.*
Merullo, Roland. *Passion for Golf.*
Palank, Ed. *The Golf Doc.*
Penick, Harvey with Bud Shrake. *Harvey Penick's Little Red Book.*
Player, Gary. *The Golfer's Guide to the Meaning of Life.*
Russell, Mark, with John Andrisani. *Golf Rules Plain and Simple.*
Sanders, Doug, with Russ Pate. *130 Different Ways to Make a Bet.*
Shapiro, Mel, Warren Dohn, and Leonard Berger, eds. *Golf: A Turn-of-the-Century Treasury.*
Snead, Sam. *How to Play Golf.*
Tatum, Frank "Sandy," Jr. *A Love Affair with the Game.*
United States Golf Association and the Royal and Ancient United States Golf Club of St. Andrews. *Decisions on the Rules of Golf, 2002–2003.*
Updike, John. *Golf Dreams.*

Vardon, Harry. *How to Play Golf.*
Wodehouse, P. G. *Divots.*

ABOUT THE AUTHORS

A student of the legendary Harvey Penick, **Barbara Puett** has introduced golf to thousands of beginning students through her golf schools and University of Texas Informal Classes. Director of Instruction for Empowered Women's Golf Schools, she is coauthor of *A Woman's Own Golf Book* (St. Martin's Press, 1999). The mother of three children, Barbara and her husband, Roane, live in Austin, Texas.

A two-time winner of Southern Texas PGA Media/Public Relations Award, author, journalist, and broadcaster **Jim Apfelbaum** is the current president of the Texas Golf Writers' Association. This is his fourth book. He has a reputation for playing the ball down and missing them quick.

Eddy Davis's stylish illustrations provided the graphic complement for *A Woman's Own Golf Book*. An accomplished golf artist, illustrator, and assistant golf professional, Eddy's work appears in private collections in the United States, Korea, and the Dutch Caribbean.

Austin American-Statesman photojournalist **Ralph Barrera** has covered Super Bowls, hurricanes, and presidential inaugurations. He's also a fine golfer, the winner of three USGA Sectional qualifiers.

Arnold Palmer and Dave Marr exiting the final green of the 1964 Masters. Palmer won by six shots. Marr finished second.
Photo courtesy of John Marr.

Page references to illustrations are in *italics*.

ace, definition of, 173
addressing the ball, 51
advice ("tips"), 8, 34, 46, 66–67, 118
apron, definition of, 173
Aragona, Joe, 120
Armour, Tommy, 108, 134, 163
Armstrong, Lance, *119*, 132
attending the flag, 84–85, 92
away
  bunkers and, 74, 76
  definition of, 52
  on the green, 88

bag drop, *25, 29*
bags
  arranging clubs in, *148*, 160
  buying, 159
  content of, 159–60
ball on flagstick, and pin position, 66, *66*
balls. *See* golf balls
Barber, Tom, 54
bare feet, 8
barkies, 127
Barton Creek Resort, *137*
Bauer, Aleck, 70
Bel-Air Country Club, 63
best ball play in tournaments, 113

Bingle, Bangle, Bongle, 127
birdie, definition of, 174
blind holes, 173
bogey, definition of, 174
Bolt, Tommy, 130
bombs, golf rules concerning, 101
Bradley, Jackson, 167
Bradley, Tina, 167
break, definition of, 83
British Isles, playing golf in, 142–46
Buffett, Warren, 125
bunkers (sand traps), 7, 71, 72, 177
  hand mashie from, 74
  loose impediments in, 74–76, 109
  manmade obstructions in, 74–76
  two players' balls in, 73–74
Burke, Jack, 79
business golf, 120–36
  host at, 122–25, 135
  packing a ditty bag for, 134–35
  talking shop in, 128, 130, 135
Byron Nelson Classic, 115

Caccamisi, Russ, 120, 127
Caen, Herb, 23

caps and hats, 22
  in British Isles, 144
carry, definition of, 172
carts, 42–47, 50–51, *110*
  electronic tracking of, 55
  not taxicabs, 56
  parking near the green by,
    79–80, 90
  repair containers on, 63
casual water, 106
cell phones, 5–6, 9, 11, 124,
    131–33, *131*, 177
charity events, 132–33
cheating, 107–8
children, 7, 10, *11*, 26, 170
chili dip (shot), 171
chipping, 10–11, 172
classified ads, *151*, 153
cleat marks on the green, 87
clothing, 14–24
  collared, 16–17, *18–19*, 19–20,
  for country clubs, 19
  of professional golfers, 22–23
  short shorts, 17–18
  women's traditional, *13*, 14
clubs. *See* country clubs; golf
    clubs
collar, definition of, 173
component clubs, 150, 153
Cook, Chuck, 169
corporate citizenship, 133
country clubs
  dress codes at, 19–20
  processing at, 28–30
  shoes at, 30
course ambassadors, 61
course rating, 96
Crenshaw, Ben, vii, 102

customer golf. *See* business
    golf

daily-fee courses. *See* semiprivate
    courses
Dalgleish, Gordon, 142–46
Darwin, Bernard, 9, 138
Decisions of the Rules of Golf,
    100, 109
deliberate golfers, 59
Demo Days, 154
distance markers, 64, *64*
divots
  definition of, 62
  repair of, 62–63, 67, 159, 177
Dixon, Patricia, 155
Dobreiner, Peter, 92
doglegs, 173
double-bogey, definition of, 174
double-eagle, definition of, 174
draw, definition of, 172
driving range, *xiv*, 1–6, *3, 5,*
    10–11
dropping in, 73–74, 104–5

eagle, definition of, 174
Empowered Women's Golf, 155
equipment, *148*, 149–61. *See also*
    specific types of equipment

fade, definition of, 172
fairway, distance markers on, 64,
    64
fan shots, 171–72
fast shots, 171
fat shots, 171
first cut, definition of, 173
first-tee introductions, 34–35

flag
  attending the, 84–85, 92
  retrieving and replacing, 90
flag colors, 66
flat shots, 171
footwear, 8, 12, 15, 21–22, 30,
  140
foot wedge, 123
"FORE!," 58
four ball play in tournaments,
  113
foursome play in tournaments,
  113
Francis, Richard, 91
free drop, 106
Friday, often considered weekend,
  27
fringe, definition of, 173

gambling. *See* wagers
"gap" wedges, 157–58
Garvey, Jeff, 132
Gates, Bill, 125
Gathright, Bryan, 168
gimmes, 89–90, 123–24, 129,
  176
Gist, Chip, 138–39, 141
Global Positioning Systems
  (GPS), 65
gloves, 159
golf bags. *See* bags
golf balls
  addressing, 51
  buying, 158
  indentations on the green by,
    80, *80*
  lost, 41, 48, 61–62, 67–68,
    104–5, 109, 161

marking of, for identification,
  40, *40*
marking of, on the green,
  86–88, *88*, 92
mishitting of, 55
picking up of, 61–62, 68, 74,
  76, 123, 136, 175
pre-shot routines for hitting, 55
provisional, 105
putting new balls into play,
  73–74, 104–5
on range, 2–3
strokes that miss, 40
unplayable, 105–6
golf clubs
  for business golf, 134
  buying one at a time, 152
  Demo Days for, 154
  four categories of, 150–51
  graphite vs. steel, 156
  grounding of, in hazards, *69*,
    70–71, 76
  labelling of, 139–40, 146
  number needed, 29
  rental, 140, 146
  shaft flex of, 154–56, *154*
  soliciting advice about, 46
  starter sets of, 153, 160
  stray, 63
  terms of description for, 173
  used sets of, 152–53
  where to buy, 149–50
Golf Course Superintendent's
  Association, 63
golf etiquette
  importance of, vii, ix, 1, 31,
    116
  least wanted list for, 177

Golf magazine, 168
golf swings
  amount of time for, 53–54
  speed of, 154–55
  terms for, 171–72
  See also practice swings
green, the, 79–92
  attending the flag on, 84–85,
    92
  collision of balls on, 85
  footwork on, 81
  indentations on, 80, *80*
  leaving, 90
  pitch and cleat marks on, 87
  putting on, 81–92
  tallying up score on, 90, 92
  through the green, definition
    of, 76
greenies, 126
Gretzky, Wayne, 34
Griffith Park, 54
gross score, 114
grounding of clubs in hazards, *69,*
  70–71, 76
ground under repair, 106

handicaps, 34, *93,* 96–98, 131,
  135
  in tournaments, 111–12
hand mashie, 74
handshakes, 33, 46, 144
Haney, Hank, 169
hazards, *69,* 70–78
  environmental, 73
  grounding of clubs in, *69,*
    70–71, 76
  hand mashie from, 74
  laying up before, 172

water, *69,* 72–73
water compared to sand, 75
See also bunkers (sand traps)
Heyde, Barbara and Jack, 21
high school golf, 117
hole locations, pin sheets for, 65,
  65
holes
  blind, 173
  dogleg, 173
  See also pin position; *specific
    holes*
honor, 38, 52
hook, definition of, 172
Hutchinson, Horace, 77, 130, 133

Intergolf Vacations, 142
Internet, 153

jingling coins, 177
Jones, Bobby, 1, 53, 75, 89, 116,
  134
junior golf, 117
junk, definition of, 126

Kite, David, 117
Kite, Tom, ix
knock-offs (clubs), 150
Knuth, Dean, 59–60

labeling of equipment, 139–40,
  146
Lahinch Golf Club, 50
lateral water hazards, *69,* 72–73
laying up, 172
Leadbetter, David, 167
lessons, *162,* 163–70
  group, 166

video, 166
what to bring to, 167–69
Locke, Bobby, 169
Longhurst, Henry, 120, 147
long shots, 171
loose impediments, 74–76, 87,
    109
Lopez, Nancy, 20
Los Angeles Country Club, 132
lost balls, 41, 48, 61–62, 67–68,
    104–5, 109, 161

marking balls
  on the green, 86–88, *88,* 92
  for identification, 40, *40*
Marr, Dave, 134, *182*
marshals, 61, 67
Martin, Judith, 58
mashie, 74
Masters tournament, 114–16, *182*
match play in tournaments, 111,
    113
medal play in tournaments, 113
medical complaints, 35
Merullo, Roland, 31
Miller, Steven L., 121, 124, 133
mishitting, 55
Miss Manners, 58
Mitchell, Abe, xi
Morris, Tom, 114
Muirfield course, 142
mulligans, 41–42, 47–48, 57,
    123–24, 132, 177
municipal courses (public courses)
  clothing for, 15–16, *16, 17*
  processing at, 28–30
  shoes at, 30
  waiting lists at, 27–28

nassaus, 126–27, 136
National Golf Foundation, 169
net score, 114
new golfers, etiquette for, 176
Nicklaus, Jack, 60, 94
90–degree rule, 44–45, *44*

odometer check, 64–65
OEM (Original Equipment
    Manufacturer) clubs, 150,
    152–53
Old Course (St. Andrews), 114,
    138
out of bounds, 104, 109

pace, 54, 59, 132
  definition of, 67
  timing statistics on, 60
packing a ditty bag, 134–35
Palmer, Arnold, *182*
par, definition of, 174
par-3 holes
  club selection on, 46
  playing through on, 57
  typical time to play, 60
  yardage markers on, *95*
par-4 holes
  bogey on, 174
  typical time to play, 60
par-5 holes
  terms for scores on, 174
  typical time to play, 60
Pebble Beach Golf Links, 16, 138
Pelz, David, 168
Penick, Harvey, xii, 134, 165–66,
    178
Perry Golf, 142
personality, golf and, 129–30, 135

PGA (Professional Golfers
    Association) Tour
  cell phones banned by, 9
  clothing for, 23–24
  Shell Houston Open, 121, 133
  slow play at, 59–60
  time allotted for shots by, 55
picking up, 61–62, 68, 74, 76,
    123, 136, 175
pin duty (attending the flag),
    84–85, 92
pin position
  ball on flagstick for, 66, *66*
  flag colors for, 66
pin sheets, 65, *65*
pitch, definition of, 172
pitching wedges, 157
pitch marks, 87, 177
Player, Gary, 26
player assistants, 61
playing it down, 125
playing through, 56–58, 67, 118
playing up, 52
practice swings, 38, 40, 55–56,
    67, 71, 103, 177
  in British Isles, 143
pre-shot routines, 55
press, the (wager), 126
pro-ams, 114–15
professional golfers
  flex shafts chosen by, 156
  marshals and assistants, 61
  in pro-ams, 114
  See also lessons; PGA
pro-line clubs, 150, 152–53, 160
provisionals, 105
public courses. *See* municipal
    courses

pull, definition of, 172
push, definition of, 172
putters
  buying, 157
  required of each player, 29
putting, 81–92
  conceding in, 89–90, 129
  continuous, 88, 92
  distractions while, 83
  retrieval of ball after, 90, 92
  silence when, 91
putting greens, 7–10, *9, 11*
putting lines, definition of, 81

rangers, 61
ready golf, 38–39, 58
relief, 106
resort golf, *137*, 138–42, 146–47
Rice, Grantland, 136
River Place course, *64*
Royal and Ancient Golf Club of
    St. Andrews (R&A)
  rule-making by, 100
Rules of Etiquette, ix
rules of golf, ix, 100–109
  basic, 101
  importance of, 101–2, 108
  local or winter rules, 125,
    174
  summer rules, 174
run, definition of, 172

safety
  on driving range, 1, 3–4, 7
  on fairway, 50, 58
  hazards and, 71
  on putting greens, 10
St. John, Lauren, 130

sandbaggers, 98
Sanders, Doug, 127
sandies, 127
sand traps. *See* bunkers
sand wedges, 157–58
scorecards, *93, 95*
  incorrect, in tournaments, 108
scores, 94–98
  gross vs. net, 114
  tallying up of, on the green, 90,
    92
  terms for, 173–74
scrambles, 112, 122, 132–33
scratch golfers, 96–97
second cut, definition of, 173
semiprivate courses
  clothing for, 16–17, *18,* 20
  processing at, 28–30
  shoes at, 30
shaft flex, 154–56, *154*
shambles, 112
shank, definition of, 172
Shell Houston Open, 121, 133
Sherrod, Blackie, 98
shoes. *See* footwear
short game, definition of, 168
short shots, 171
shotgun start, 174
side bets, 126–27
skins, 127–28
skulled shot, 171
sky, definition of, 172
slice, definition of, 172
slope index, 95
slow play, xi, 54–55, 59, 67–68,
    114
  marshals and, 61, 67
slow shots, 171

smoking, 45
Snead, Sam, 14
sprinkler head plaques, 64
Stableford play in tournaments,
    113
Stacy, Hollis, 20
starters, 30
statistics on golfers in U.S., 169
sticks and leaves, lifting of,
    74–76, 87
store-line clubs, 150, 153
Stringer, Mabel E., 14
stroke and distance, 104, 109
stroke play in tournaments, 111
Stroke Saver, 140
stroke-team events, 97
summer rules, 174
Sweden, tests for golfers in, 2, 12

taking a drop, 73–74, 104–5
tap-ins, 89
Tatum, Frank "Sandy," Jr., 94
teeing ground (tee box). *See* tees
tees
  mulligans and, 41–42
  rules for, 40, 103
  selecting, 36–37
tee times, 27–28, 140–41, 146
temper, displays of, 130
thin shot, 171
Thomson, Peter, 70
through the green, definition of,
    76
tipping
  of attendants, 29
  in British Isles, 142, 144–45
  at resorts, 139, 146
  for shining street shoes, 30

topped shot, 171
Tour de France, *119,* 132
tournaments, 111–18
  business, 131
  cheating in, 107–8
  crowd behavior at, 116
  match play in, 111
  scrambles, 112, 122, 132–33
  shambles, 112
  shotgun starts in, 174
  stroke (or medal) play in, 111,
    113
traps. *See* bunkers
trash, definition of, 126
trees as no cause of relief, 106
Tremeer, Steve, 138–39, 141
Trevino, Lee, 127
triple-bogey, definition of, 174
"turn," the (end of first nine
  holes), playing through at, 57
turn taking, *49,* 50–52
  on the green, 82, 88
  waiting your turn, *32, 39,* 47,
    51
turtles, 59
Twain, Mark, 161
twilight fees, 26–27

UCLA (University of California at
  Los Angeles), 63
unplayable lies, 105–6
Updike, John, 54
upright shots, 171
USGA (United States Golf
  Association), ix
  handicap card of, 96
  rule books of, 109
  rule-making by, 100

Valderrama course, 21
valuables, stowing of, 141
Vardon, Harry, 149

wagers, 102, 107, 125–28
waiting lists, 27–28
waiting your turn, *32, 39,* 47,
  51
Waldorf, Duffy, 40
Ward-Thomas, Pat, 41
water, casual, 106
water hazards, *69,* 72–73
Watson, Tom, 104
wedges, 157–58
whiffs, 171–72
Whigham, H. J., 68, 111
winter rules, 125, 174
Wodehouse, P. G., 34, 91
Wolf (choosing sides),
  127–28
women
  average score of, 169
  on British courses, 146
  in business golf, 122
  golf clubs for, 155–56
  golf clothing for, *13,* 14,
    16–21, *16, 19,* 23
  handicaps for, 97
  and slow play, *59*
  teeing off by, 37
Woods, Tiger, 116
woods (golf clubs), 157
wormburners, 171

X-outs (golf balls), 158, 160

yardage, 64–65, 67
yardage books, 140, 146